Waiting for the Wonder

Waiting for the Wonder

Voices of Advent

Katerina Katsarka Whitley

morehouse

HARRISBURG • LONDON

Morehouse Publishing, P.O. Box 1321, Harrisburg, PA 17105

Morehouse Publishing, The Tower Building, 11 York Road, London SE1 7NX

Morehouse Publishing is a Continuum imprint.

Cover design: Wesley Hoke

Cover art: *The Annunciation* by Henry Ossawa Tanner. Philadelphia Museum of Art: Purchased with the W. P. Wilstach Fund, 1899.

Library of Congress Cataloging-in-Publication Data

Whitley, Katerina Katsarka.
    Waiting for the wonder : voices of Advent /
Katerina Katsarka Whitley.
        p. cm.
    ISBN 0-8192-2125-2 (pbk.)
    1. Advent—Prayer-books and devotions—English.
2. Devotional calendars. I. Title.
BV40.W48 2005
242'.332—dc22   2005000305

Printed in the United States of America

05   06   07   08   09   10   6   5   4   3   2   1

With love to my grandchildren, who live in wonder

Alexandra
Luke
Jeremy
Miles

Contents

Prologue: O come, Emmanuel ix

Amos: Let justice roll like waters 1

Micah: The prophet's lament and his dream of peace 4

Isaiah: The comfort of a child from a Father who despairs
of his children 7

Ruth: Waiting for the wonder 10

David: Youthful dream of love 14

The Zealot: Desire for revenge 17

A Roman: The young centurion and a friend 20

The Archangel: Gabriel addresses the host of heaven 24

The Lesser Angels: Our song 27

Zechariah: The visitation 29

Elizabeth and Mariam: In the hill country 32

Joseph: A visit from Mariam and the angel Gabriel 35

Anna: The news my daughter brought me 38

Joachim: A father's shock and recognition 42

Mariam's Childhood Friend: Sharing secrets in Nazareth 45

A Barren Woman: Waiting in Bethlehem, in ordinary time ... 49

Mariam: The Virgin contemplates the words of her song 53

A Midwife: Journeying to Bethlehem with a swallow for
company 56

The Shepherd Father: Abiding in the fields 60

Jonathan: The shepherd boy and the night sky 63

The Lamb: Jonathan's lamb meets the Lamb of God 66

The Donkey: Its burden and its story 70

The Babylonian *Magos*: Reading the stars and planets 73

King Herod: His troubled dreams 78

The Greek *Magos*: Escaping Herod's clutches 81

The Innkeeper's Granddaughter: A story from Bethlehem 85

Symeon: He waits for the promise and is not disappointed 89

Anna the Prophet: Her last words 91

Luke: The evangelist's last story 94

James: A brother tells his story 97

Epilogue: The end of one season, the beginning of another 101

Prologue
O come, Emmanuel

*I believe that I shall see the goodness of the LORD
in the land of the living.* (Psalm 27:13)

Anticipation—Advent

To wait. To hope. To dream. We share these human longings—
we creatures of the Almighty.

A memory from earliest childhood visits me. I am lying in
bed—a restless child whose mind doesn't easily turn off. Outside
the bedroom door is the sitting room, in that small apartment in
Thessaloniki, in the middle of the war years. My parents are talking quietly to one another. The sound is comforting. Whenever
I'm in distress, because of fever or a bad dream, I know that door
will open and Daddy will appear to say quietly—*Don't be afraid.*
Despite the dark, I'm waiting for something good because someone who loves me is on the other side of that door.

In the dark again, in bed, I hear the sirens howling outside.
The airplanes will arrive soon and the bombs will start falling. A
sliver of light appears under the door. I know that when the door
opens that faint light will enter together with my father, and the
light will enlarge to disperse the darkness. I already recognize,
young as I am, that the light has the power to do this—to disperse
the darkness—but I also know that the dark can never overcome
the light in the same manner. If there is even a dot of light I can
focus on that and all will be well. Together with the light comes

my father and the security of his presence. *My children, do not be afraid. We are in God's hands.*

Advent—anticipation

O blessed day, come!

I have lived in the States for seven and a half years, alone, without my family, with only friends and teachers and strangers for five years, and then with my husband and, more recently, my infant daughter. I am ready to return home to Greece, after the long, long years of absence. No matter how many times I will return after this first trip back, nothing will ever again compare to the excitement, the unadulterated joy that says, *I am going home, I am going home.* Oh, the joy of anticipation: to see my loved ones again, the apartment where I grew up, the tiny church hall where I worshiped and learned to trust and learned to create. Oh, to be home in Greece again. The delicious, indescribable expectancy of return.

Anticipation—being reunited with joy

1964. My husband has been in Vietnam for a whole, agonizing year. The telegram has finally arrived. He is coming home to Greece to see his wife and child again. My husband, my little daughter, and I will be a family once again. The sweetness of knowing he is alive, he is safe—we will be together again!

Thank you, God, thank you for mercy.

The memories are mine but the emotions are familiar to everyone. We recognize them. We know what it means to anticipate. There is a sweetness in waiting for the wonder that nothing can equal, sometimes not even the satisfaction of expectations being fulfilled.

This book springs from the conviction that we all long to see the "goodness of the Lord in the land of the living," that the Creator responded to the most profound longing in human beings with a specific event, in a specific time, in a particular place. Incarnation. Those who waited for the wonder of God's coming to us in our human form were not disappointed.

O come, O come, Emmanuel.

Let us prepare together to welcome Emmanuel—God with us.

Amos

Let justice roll like waters

The lion has roared;
who will not fear?
The Lord GOD has spoken;
who can but prophesy? (Amos 3:8)

For lo, the one who forms the mountains, creates the wind,
reveals his thoughts to mortals,
makes the morning darkness,
and treads on the heights of the earth—
the LORD, the God of hosts, is his name! (Amos 4:13)

. . . prepare to meet your God. . . . (Amos 4:12b)

I was keeping my sheep in the highlands of Tekoa when the word of the Lord came to me and plucked me from my place to throw me before the unjust within the city walls. The sheep were better company, the earth a more welcome bed for me. But the Lord spoke, and I obeyed.

Those I met along the way praised the king and listed all the gifts of the land as rewards of power and victory. We are a prosperous nation, they told me. Our women sleep on ivory beds, they claimed. Our military is powerful, no one can defeat us, they shouted.

I continued on my way, already sick at heart about their flagrant misunderstanding of the Lord's words. The chief priest bragged about the attention lavished on their festivals and the wealth offered in sacrifices. His pride assaulted my ears. Then the Lord loosened my tongue and I proclaimed God's judgment.

> Thus says the LORD:
> For three transgressions of Israel,
> and for four, I will not revoke the punishment;
> because they sell the righteous for silver,
> and the needy for a pair of sandals—
> they who trample the head of the
> poor into the dust of the earth,
> and push the afflicted out of the way. . .

I persisted under the heavy burden of prophecy. I saw their misdeeds, I witnessed their sin, and I could not find it in my heart to beg the Lord's forgiveness for them. For they had forgotten their Lord, the One who brought them out of Egypt. Convinced that on *the day of the Lord* they would be redeemed and forgiven, they closed their ears to my words. And then the surprise sent from God stunned even me. I cried it out to them in order to warn them:

> Is not the day of the LORD darkness, not light,
> and gloom with no brightness in it?

I bent in two under the weight of that darkness and asked my Lord for a sign of hope. The people's songs hit my ears like noise; there was no melody left in the harp. I turned away from the people to the countryside I loved; I left the city to walk by the River Jordan, and as I climbed the hills I came upon a rock split in two, fierce water rushing from its crack. And I knew what mattered to the Lord. I raised my voice and cried out,

> Let justice roll down like waters,
> and righteousness like an ever-flowing stream.

They refused to listen but sent their high priest to the gate to keep me out of the city. I returned to my sheep and could not harden my heart but shed my tears for those who had turned away from their God. I prayed for a ray of light, I prayed for the salvation of the people. God sent me a dream filled with light, a promise to bestow on those who recognize justice:

> On that day I will raise up
> the booth of David that is fallen,
> and repair its breaches,
> and raise up its ruins,
> and rebuild it as in the days of old. . . .

And in my dream, out there on the hillside, surrounded only by my sheep, I saw that *all the nations* were blessed by this return to the Light, and those who called upon the Lord in justice and peace were not ignored or abandoned. The sheep and I wait on the Lord.

Micah
The prophet's lament
and his dream of peace

And he shall stand and feed his flock in the strength of the
LORD. . .
and he shall be the one of peace. (Micah 5:4a, 5a)

In the small village of Moresbeth—no glories of Jerusalem here—
I have known from earliest years that my tongue has been touched
by the hand of the Lord my God, together with my heart and
spirit.

I spoke in verse as a child and my parents marveled and were
afraid. The visions came unasked for and found words on my lips.
So I knew from childhood on that I must pay attention.

What I noticed troubled me and shook me to the depths of
my being. I found myself weeping whenever I saw the rich
oppressing the poor and those who were fed taking food away
from the hungry. And I vowed to the Lord that I would speak out
against injustice even if it meant the end of my own life.

And I said:
Listen, you heads of Jacob
and rulers of the house of Israel!
Should you not know justice?—
you who hate the good and love the evil,
who tear the skin off my people,
and the flesh off their bones. . .

4

But they listened to false prophets instead, to those who promised them success and prosperity saying, "Surely the Lord is with us! No harm shall come upon us." Thus says the Lord concerning these false prophets

> who cry "Peace" when they have something to eat,
>> but declare war against those who put nothing
>>> into their mouths. . . .
>> The sun shall go down upon the prophets,
>> and the day shall be black over them. . . .

But they loved war more than peace, while I dreamed in vain of my former friends sitting under their own vines and under their own fig trees.

I became like a madman in my travels to sinful Jerusalem, walking naked and barefoot, trying to call the unjust to the One who laments over them:

> "O my people, what have I done to you?
> In what have I wearied you?
> Answer me!"

I struggled to remind them of the mercies of our God throughout our long history. And still they asked only about sacrifices and burnt offerings: *Will the Lord be pleased with thousands of rams? with ten thousands of rivers of oil?* I left Jerusalem to return to my humble village and to the people I loved, away from the rulers and the faithless prophets. And it was as I was passing through Bethlehem that I found consolation. God blessed me with a vision of mercy, of a shepherd who cares for his flock, of a king like no other.

> And he shall stand and feed his flock
> in the strength of the LORD,
> in the majesty of the name of
> the LORD his God.

And to Bethlehem I sang:

> But you, O Bethlehem of Ephrathah,
> who are one of the little clans of Judah,
> from you shall come forth for me
> one who is to rule in Israel,
> whose origin is from of old,
> from ancient days.

And those who heard me rejoiced but they forgot to stand, to wait and hear how to receive him. For none of this can come to pass—the beating of their swords into plowshares, and their spears into pruning hooks—without the fullness of the Word. Without a clean heart they cannot achieve God's dream that "nation shall not lift up sword against nation, neither shall they learn war any more," for the mouth of the Lord has spoken it, if only they would listen.

> He has told you, O mortal, what is good;
> and what does the LORD require of you
> but to do justice, and to love kindness,
> and to walk humbly with your God?

And in my grief and sorrow, I looked to the One who shall come from humble Bethlehem, not with drawn sword, nor with armies, but with justice and peace, to fulfill the Lord's promise. For

> who is a God like you, pardoning iniquity
> and passing over the transgression?

I know a God who

> does not retain his anger forever,
> because he delights in showing clemency.
> He will again have compassion upon us. . . .

I wait on the Lord.

Isaiah
The comfort of a child from a Father who despairs of his children

The wolf shall live with the lamb,
the leopard shall lie down with the kid,
the calf and the lion and the fatling together,
and a little child shall lead them. (Isaiah 11:6)

The visions troubled me to the point of agony. Some called it madness, and they may have been right. I reached the edge again and again, poised between sanity and madness in my sorrow for the people who have forsaken the Lord, who have despised the Holy One and are estranged from the One who loves them. The smell of their burnt offering in my nostrils, I looked to the heavens and heard the voice of the Lord saying,

> I have had enough of burnt offerings of rams. . .
> bringing offerings is futile;
> incense is an abomination to me.

But after the darkness brought on by the assemblies with iniquity that have become a burden to the Lord there arrived this vision, and its coming was a balm: sweet as honey, tender as a mother's love, comforting as my father's hand in mine when I was a young child. The vision was imbued with light. This light has never been extinguished, though other, darker visions followed it.

Through the many years that have rolled into oblivion since then, I have heard the pundits and the would-be prophets trying to interpret my vision, to understand it. Now that I am old, I know that most human interpretations of visions are wrong. How do we capture the Divine within the human mind? And how does the song of heaven touch the strings of our lyre? I too have sought to understand and have given voice to my visions. Many of them have been fulfilled in my lifetime. But this one vision I have only felt. I never sought to understand it, for its comfort was so welcome that I resisted putting it into words. I only wanted to live in it, to breathe it, and to continue feeling its comfort as I felt it the first time it appeared to me. These are the only words I found, and so far in my lifetime, no one has understood them as they were meant:

> For unto us a child is born,
> unto us a son is given.

Why should they have filled me with such joy? They came to me from a God who had despaired of the love of his own children. My tears ran profusely as I wrote of God's unfathomable heartache:

> I reared children and brought them up,
> but they have rebelled against me.

Is there a hurt more searing than that caused by ungrateful, unloving children? And the vision continued in its excruciating pain:

> What more was there to do for my vineyard
> that I have not done in it?
> When I expected it to yield grapes,
> why did it yield wild grapes?

The images continued to fill me with despair, to flood me with God's grief. And then, when I had given up hope for any comfort, came these tender words: *"Look, the young woman is with child and shall bear a son, and shall name him Immanuel."* Ah, the goodness of that thought—God with us. And then it became more certain—this hope of a coming—but of a child? From a God who had despaired of his children's love? Who is this child? I cried to the Lord.

The voice answered:

> Authority rests upon his shoulder;
> and he is named
> Wonderful Counselor, Mighty God,
> Everlasting Father, Prince of Peace. . . .

I cried out: *Mighty God?* Is it possible that God is talking about the Godself in the form of a child?

But I received no answer that I could understand. Only a song in my ears rang its joyful news:

> The people who walked in darkness
> have seen a great light;
> those who lived in a land of deep darkness—
> on them light has shined.

I had to be content with that. I prayed that I would see that day. But now, at the end of my days, I am still waiting, praying that those who will walk in light will recognize the Giver of light. Come, Immanuel, come!

Ruth
Waiting for the wonder

Why have I found favor in your sight,
that you should take notice of me,
when I am a foreigner? (Ruth 2:10b)

May you produce children in Ephrathah and bestow a name
in Bethlehem; and, through the children that the LORD will
give you by this young woman. . . . (Ruth 4:11b–12a)

They named him Obed; he became the father of Jesse, the father
of David. (Ruth 4:17b)

. . . and Salmon the father of Boaz by Rahab, and Boaz the
father of Obed by Ruth, and Obed the father of Jesse, and Jesse
the father of King David. . . . (Matthew 1:5–6)

It was a night of personal terror and unconcealed shame. Imagine what it felt like. Imagine being tutored by your own mother-in-law on how to seduce a man. I had been a widow for a couple of years. I had left all I had known as a girl—my parents, my village, my traditions—to enter the alien world of the Hebrew children. I did it because Naomi, my dead husband's mother, was a powerful presence in my life, and because nothing could be the same for me in Moab now that my foreign husband is dead. I would be an outcast at home as the widow of a Jew. So I decided to follow Naomi across the border, and even she thought I was a fool to do so. But she was lonely and, bereft of all three men in her life—her husband Elimelech and her sons Mahlon and Chilion—she was glad for my company.

Together we returned to Bethlehem, her village and the ancestral home of her husband's family. Everyone there seemed to know her, but I was sad that she felt such bitterness at returning with only one daughter-in-law instead of the triumph she had envisioned—coming home with her husband, her sons and grandsons. Again, I felt that I didn't count.

By now everyone seems to know my story, but I want to tell you about my night of terror and shame. I had been gleaning the fields because I didn't want Naomi to starve and, young as I was, I thought, *Maybe one of the young reapers will see me and choose me for a wife.* How else was I to survive? As I bent down to pick up the leavings of others I kept thinking how sad life was for women. We were prey to every man's desire. If we had no man to protect us we became things to be grabbed and claimed, not human beings to be cherished. I remember my tears as I walked behind the reapers, tears that never stopped. I felt that life was unfair, but I was not selfish enough to think this was my fate alone. I could see that it was the fate of all women. I would ask, *Why, why are we fated to be things and not persons? Who is this god of the Israelites? They seem to think this god really cares for them.* To me that became an ever-present question: *Who is this god of the people of Bethlehem?*

As I worked, I was terrified that someone would assault me— any man could do so, any man could have me just for the taking. And that knowledge filled me with unbearable despair and fear. So, the moment the day's work was finished, I would hide myself among the other gleaners, my head completely covered with only my eyes free so that I could see my feet as they trudged along, and I would rush back to the security of severe Naomi who would fight anyone to protect me.

Every day I followed the gleaners because they knew best which fields were ready for harvest and which reapers were merciful enough to leave some barley on the stalks and on the ground for us poor migrants. We lived in a world where the rich knew only the rich, and the poor associated only with the poor. I was learning the life of the very poor. But God had other plans for me.

One evening, when I stopped to ease my aching back, I let my shawl fall off my head for just a moment so that a breeze would cool my brow. And it was at that moment that I heard a voice call out to the reapers, *The Lord be with you,* and they answered, *The Lord bless you.* I was so stunned by this greeting, by the bearing of the man himself, that I forgot to cover my hair and my face. And that is when Boaz saw me. I shared all this with Naomi and she started thinking that this encounter had been sent from God and she decided to help God's plan along.

The rest has entered the realm of storytelling in Bethlehem, my son tells me. Grandmothers tell the story to their children and mothers to their young. But they don't know how terrified I was.

Boaz made himself known to me, but he was being kind to a poor foreign girl. It was Naomi who saw a future in this encounter. It was she who told me to lie down with Boaz when he rested on the threshing floor. I was obedient to my mother-in-law, but I knew how far-fetched her idea was. Boaz would take me in the night, and then he would discard me. I made myself beautiful—that's what Naomi called me. She coached me, she told me what to do, and Boaz would do the rest, she told me. I did as I was instructed, but I felt that death would be better than this plot of seduction.

Boaz stirred in the night and found me there, sleeping next to him. He was astounded but respectful and very kind, and that changed everything for me. After he left me to sleep without shame, I had a dream; this is what no one else knows. The dream was sent from God. This much I know. It said: *Do not be afraid, but wait for the goodness of the Lord, in this land of Bethlehem.* After that night I no longer felt an alien—I knew that this God I longed to know cared for people like me also, a foreigner and a woman.

The dream unfolded in Bethlehem. It was full of promise. I thought it was foretelling the future of my son, but of that I am not certain. Someone has told me that a year is like a moment in the eyes of God, so what I saw may not come to pass while my children are living, but it will come to pass. In my dream I saw a place just like Bethlehem where women followed a good man who taught them about his God and honored them as full human beings. I thought, *Ah, my sons will be good to women and cherish them.* I heard this good man teaching peace and I saw him practicing mercy. I thought, *Naomi and Boaz have given me hints of a good God, I will listen to them.* And in my dream I knew that this good man blessed the name of Bethlehem forever and ever and that I was one of his ancestors.

I never forgot my dream. I have taught its lessons to my first-born Obed and to all the children that followed. The God of my people here in Bethlehem is a God of mercy who has compassion even for foreigners. I wake up every morning waiting to see God's goodness in every day. I tell my children, *Wait for the wonder; it will come to you as it has come to me.*

David
Youthful dream of love

And whenever the evil spirit. . . came upon Saul, David took the lyre and played it with his hand, and Saul would be relieved and feel better, and the evil spirit would depart from him. (1 Samuel 16:23)

So the All Great, were the All-Loving too—
So, through the thunder comes a human voice
Saying, "O heart I made, a heart beats here!
Face my hands fashioned, see it in myself!"
(Robert Browning, *An Epistle*, lines 305–8)

Do I find love so full in my nature, God's ultimate gift,
That I doubt his own love can compete with it?
Here, the parts shift?
Here, the creature surpass the Creator,—the end, what Began?
(Robert Browning, *Saul*, lines 267–69)

I have been a good king. A great king. Lying here on this cold bed in my old skin that nothing can restore, not even the warmth of another human being, surrounded by those who think me already dead, unable to think or to remember, *I do remember.*

God has loved me. No one in the history of our people has been as favored and loved by the Lord. Yet, after so many wives and children and wars and victories, I am lying here recalling only my youth, the years of being a shepherd, the carefree, delicious years of innocence. It is easier to think of those years than all the mistakes I made as king—the children I have lost, my beloved Absalom, the shame of his sister Tamar, and the murder of Amnon, my firstborn who abused her. How much of all this was my fault? I remember what I did to Bathsheba's husband, the infant who died as a result of my sin, and I worry about Bathsheba's other son, Solomon. Is he the right one to succeed me?

I prefer remembering those heady days when Samuel anointed me to succeed Saul. What a happy youth I was with my sheep, my lyre, my songs, the sounds of the waters, the trills of the birds, the whisper of the wind among the leaves, the lambs calling for their mothers—ah, those were the times when I knew joy.

I remember Saul and his darkness, the madness that came over him, my own love for him despite all his efforts to destroy me, and my great love for Jonathan, the beloved friend of my heart. Where have all these feelings gone? What happens to our loves, to our songs, to good conversations, to prayers and psalms to God? What happens to them? Do they disappear into the air, never to return?

Lost in the regrets of my mind and the chill of my aged skin, I call on God to have mercy on me for I have been a sinner. And the All-Merciful sends me a memory that fills me with such joy that now, finally, I am ready to die in peace. If only I had the power to write it down so that everyone who comes after me could read it, hold on to it, and wait for the Lord's anointed.

I was singing to Saul on that terrible day when he threw his javelin at me to impale me against the wall. I had been singing of the beauty of the world, the joy of running in the fields, the flight of birds, the sounds of the waters, the majesty of the storms. But I was not getting through to his troubled mind. After he tried to kill me, I wondered: *How is it that I love you, Saul, when all you want to do is destroy me? Who is it who fills me with such love? How is it possible that I can love you when you hate me?* And it was then that

I had this assurance—forgotten all these many years, but now here again to comfort me and to lead me gently back to my Creator. In answer to my questions I was sent the vision of the One who was with God before the world began: "You are my son, this day I have begotten you." The song filled my being and overflowed. I saw the human form of the beloved of God and I asked, "Is this how you will come to us?" and the answer was there before me—the Face of God's anointed, the love that surpasses all other loves. This vision was a gift beyond my power to achieve, beyond my capacity of knowing, yet still a gift I grasped in my youth. Now lying here on this cold bed I remember that time of great blessedness: knowing that *I loved* and *why* I loved.

The one who fashioned me and shaped me in God's image also taught me how to love. Oh, my people, don't lose heart. Wait, wait for the Lord's anointed.

The Zealot
Desire for revenge

How long, O LORD? Will you be angry forever?
Will your jealous wrath burn like fire?
Pour out your anger on the nations
that do not know you,
and on the kingdoms
that do not call on your name. (Psalm 79:5–6)

I spend my days pouring over the words of psalmists and prophets, looking for the Messiah of Israel. I want him to be full of power, a mighty counselor who will deliver us from the enemy. That is all. I am not looking for a king; I am not looking for a savior. I only want a deliverer.

O that you would kill the wicked, O God,
and that the bloodthirsty would depart from me—
those who speak of you maliciously,
and lift themselves up against you for evil!
Do I not hate those who hate you, O LORD?
And do I not loathe those who rise up against you?
I hate them with perfect hatred;
I count them my enemies.

You shall break them with a rod of iron,
and dash them in pieces like a potter's vessel.

17

I keep reading these words from the psalms and can't get enough of them. Not for me the peaceful scenes of Isaiah's paradise. Not for me the one who defends the poor and the widow. What I long for is an avenger. The Romans were responsible for the death of my father, and the Romans must die. This is my hope—to kill as many as possible before they kill me, and to oust them from this land.

Is this too much to ask of a God who favors us, who favors Israel? Were we not called to be the chosen people? Was not a promise given to David that his descendants would rule the earth?

The signs are pointing to the destruction of the Romans and those who collaborate with them. I was talking to one of Herod's scribes yesterday and he said that Herod was growing weaker by the hour and his sickness was eating his flesh. I hear that there are rumors among the Roman soldiers that their Augustus will not live much longer. So this is the time to strike. I am storing weapons. I am saying to everyone who will listen that open rebellion, open war is the only way to live and to die. This is what I'm waiting for: victory over oppression! It is the only thing that matters—and the privilege of defending the name of our God, for we are the ones who are doing God's bidding. Destroy the enemy! So let Messiah hurry his coming. All we need to do is be prepared.

My pious brother tells me I am mad. He reminds me that most of the prophets proclaimed a just God who looks with favor on those who do justice, not on those who make war. Let him have his God and I will have mine, I say. My brother is a fool. He is waiting for a savior who will reveal God's character to us. I look back through our history and I see countless wars and battles, and I believe this is the only language that enemies understand and the only one that makes sense to us. Isaiah and Micah had it wrong. Only power is understood and respected on this earth. Look at the Romans. Learn from them, I say. Did they ever back down before an enemy? Did they use "compassion" and "mercy" in dealing with those who stood up against them? No, they used the sword. The sword brings justice with it. So let us learn to use the sword also. It is with violence that we impose our will on others; patience and peacemaking show us up as weaklings. I will never again be weak. I have been turning the words of the psalmist inside out:

> For in my bow do I trust
> And my sword will save me.

Come, deliverer of Israel. Come, warrior lord. I am waiting and I am ready.

A Roman
The young centurion and a friend

A shoot shall come out from the stump of Jesse,
and a branch shall grow out of his roots.
The spirit of the LORD shall rest on him. . . .
His delight shall be in the fear of the LORD.
They will not hurt or destroy
on all my holy mountain;
for the earth shall be full of the
knowledge of the LORD
as the waters cover the sea. (Isaiah 11:1–2a, 3, 9)

Now there was a Pharisee named Nicodemus, a leader of the
Jews. He came to Jesus by night. . . . (John 3:1–2a)

Rome is the queen who reigns supreme. We have defeated and surpassed even the glory of Athens. I look at those who are not Romans and I pity them. I begin each morning with this declamation: How good it is to be alive and to be a Roman.

For many months I have been filled with anger that I am obligated to serve my time away from Rome, away from the Forum and its magnificent space and the temples that adorn our city. On the days when I am most homesick, I walk to Herod's Temple just to see its grandeur and to remember Rome. I don't like Jerusalem. I don't like her people, and I resent every moment

I spend here. I find the Jews arrogant despite their poverty and their status as residents of an occupied land. It is their religion I resent the most—their conviction that only they know the one true god. As if one god could ever suffice for the many different peoples on this earth! As if their god could possibly be greater than the gods of the Romans. Who is it who favors them? If indeed their god is the greatest of gods, why are they not the most powerful people on earth?

These are the questions that troubled and irritated me before I met the one friend I have made in this land. On a day when I fumed about my posting, I found myself walking near Herod's Temple to see its marble and gold, though I longed for Roman columns and arches. As I stood watching and thinking, one of their learned men, a perceptive young student, noticed me and approached to offer me his companionship. It surprised me so much that I almost dismissed him, but then I noticed his smiling eyes and the scrolls under his arm and decided to take the chance, just this once, of getting to know one of these Jews as a person, not only as a poor subject of the empire. He said, "Why don't you walk with me to the Mount of Olives? I have seen you here many a day and recognize that you are restless and unhappy. I would be also, were I in your position." That understanding disarmed me immediately. He continued, "Let me tell you something about this Temple and this land of ours with its long, long history and its repeated wars and occupations. You may be surprised at what you learn."

Thus it was that we became friends. His name is Nicodemus—from all appearances a wealthy young man who is studying to be a lawyer, one of the class known as Pharisees. Since I too was a student of the ancients before becoming a soldier of the empire, a centurion, I decided to take him up on his offer. Ever since that day I find myself filled with questions that I must spend a lifetime examining. Nicodemus, with his keen mind and skeptical nature, has proved to be a delightful companion. (I don't share this with any of my fellow soldiers for fear they will laugh at me.)

He is a marvelous storyteller. He tells me about his people's great patriarch Abraham and some of his famous descendants. What has struck me with a force I had not expected was the recounting of a covenant between their god and specific men of their race. It is a new idea for me and I have to spend much time trying to examine it. The covenant has profound roots, not like the superficial bargains we strike up with the Olympians and the gods of the Pantheon. The story that has captured my fancy recalls their great king, David, a poet warrior. "Hmm," I say, "our own Caesar was a man of letters; the Greeks' own great general Pericles was a brilliant man of words also. I had no idea you had a tradition of learning going so far back into history." He smiles whenever I make such comments. He has started telling me about the wise men of the Israel of old, known as prophets rather than seers. "What did they foretell?" I ask, but he shakes his head. "Their role is to call us to justice," he answers, "not to foretell the future."

This intrigues me. I want to know more. What kind of justice? "God's justice," he says, and uses the Greek word *dikaiosyne*. Not revenge. He tells me the words of a serious poet called Isaiah, using the Greek translation of his words since I don't know Hebrew. "The deep, rich sound of the Greek," he says, "comes close to the beauty of the Hebrew." He recites:

> Seek justice,
> correct oppression;
> defend the fatherless,
> plead for the widow.

"This is what God's justice is about," Nicodemus explains, and I tell him that even though the thoughts are alien to a Roman they fill me with longing for something better for the world. My new friend now surprises me. "Listen," he says, "you were asking about foretelling the future, and it is possible that this vision is for a time yet to come. Our prophets have written about a fervent hope for the world, about a savior who will bring peace, who will correct injustice." I am confused but I long to know about this hope. He recites:

> He shall judge between the nations,
>   and shall arbitrate for many peoples;
> they shall beat their swords into plowshares,
>   and their spears into pruning hooks;
> nation shall not lift up sword against nation,
>   neither shall they learn war any more.

"I would be out a job then," I say, making a joke, because my whole being longs to take these words seriously. My friends would laugh with derision if they heard such a speech. But I am strangely moved and long for the coming of the one who can bring this kind of peace to the nations. Nicodemus says, "Such peace may not be possible; the Jews' most fervent hope is for the Messiah, God's anointed, who will deliver us from the Roman yoke."

He looks at me to gauge my reaction, but I don't let him know how angry his words make me. After all, I admit to myself, I would not want to live in an occupied land either.

I leave him and return to the barracks to think. In my hands I hold a tablet on which I have copied these words from his prophet: *and the wolf shall live with the lamb, and a little child shall lead them.*

I tremble as one does when a premonition hits accurately. All I can do is wait.

The Archangel
Gabriel addresses the host of heaven

*In the beginning was the Word, and the Word was with God, and the
Word was God. He was in the beginning with God.* (John 1:1–2)

*And being found in human form, he humbled himself and became
obedient to the point of death.* (Philippians 2:7–8)

*Then I heard every creature in heaven and on earth and under the
earth and in the sea, and all that is in them, singing,
"To the one seated on the throne and to the Lamb
be blessing and honor and glory and might
forever and ever!"* (Revelation 5:13)

Holy creatures of the Almighty, behold! A new world is coming.
A new creation is being born.

Companions of Deep Heaven, attend to my words! I have
entered the other realm repeatedly in this past cycle of the earth, the
one the other creatures of the Almighty call Time, the realm human
beings inhabit. I, Gabriel, who stand at the right hand of God,
became the messenger of the Most High—blessed be God's Holy
Name—to people of humble birth and pure hearts. At first I found
it mysterious that the Almighty had chosen to send me to such an
obscure place, east of the sea earth-people call the Mediterranean.
Troubled nations live all around it, and there is trouble within it.

I had expected I would be sent to the Greeks, whose wisdom has reached such heights that we have marveled at how close they have come to the Truth at times; or to the Romans, whose cleverness, persistence, and strength have propelled them throughout much of the earth, as they know it, and has made them powerful in their eyes; or to those farther east who have achieved so much of beauty. But the Almighty sent me instead to what seemed like a hovel. To a girl of such inner loveliness, obedience, and courage that even I felt a momentary surprise.

I announced to her the news of the Coming, and she bent her head and said yes. Her family calls her Mariam. She did not know what scorn would be heaped upon her; the people of the earth don't understand the gentleness of the All-Merciful, blessed be God's Name. They seem to sense the Creator only in huge disasters that shake up their earth, but they never seem to see God's hand in the tenderness of life. She does not suspect that people will elevate her beyond the human, does not recognize that God has found her worthy precisely because of her humanity. But, in human time, all that is to come.

I brought the good news to Mariam soon after bringing a similar message to her cousin Elizabeth, and this was a surprise even to me, the servant of the Most High. I was sent first to her husband, one of the priests who serve in the earthly Temple, and he laughed so hard, he lost his voice as a result of his inability to believe in my words. But his wife received the news with humility, and she, together with Mariam, has rejoiced within God's favor. They understand the gentleness of the All-Merciful.

Their time has come. Elizabeth has given birth to a strong son, but I have seen some of you approaching what human beings call sorrow and weeping because you are able to see his end. Do not grieve (to use a human term) for the Pródromos—the one who goes before to prepare the way. He will accomplish his mission and remain very close to the heart of the Most Holy.

And now the will of the Eternal is being fulfilled in a place so humble and obscure that people will debate, argue, talk, and write about it for thousands of the segmented spans of time they call years. I am offering permission to as many of you as are willing to enter the other realm to approach the infant, only on this night, so that you may rejoice with his parents. And to give you comfort, since I sense that you are disappointed not to have been chosen for this mission. The Creator—blessed be God's Holy Name—has chosen only human beings for this central event in all creation.

I feel your amazement. It is as a *human infant* that the Almighty is entering the human realm. You do well to fall down and worship. Your awe is felt throughout the universe. But we, we do not have the human capacity for tears or for laughter. We can only sing the praises of the Most Holy, and we must wait.

I forbid you from entering the other realm for any purpose other than to offer praise to the Most High, who has willed this fearful thing to come to pass. You are not allowed to assist this infant in any way, and you will not be able to do so after his years of infancy have passed. *He is to live the life of man.* The awe, the near fear that grips us at the thought of his human passage and of his coming suffering is understandable. But we have been forbidden from interference. We do not understand the will of the Most High, blessed is God's Holy Name. Together with the young maiden who said yes to God, we must also say yes and await the fulfillment of the Creator's holy purpose.

Amen and amen and amen.

The Lesser Angels
Our song

"I am the Alpha and the Omega," says the Lord God, who is and who was and who is to come, the Almighty. (Revelation 1:8)

The people that walked in darkness have seen a great light: they that dwell in the land of the shadow of death, upon them hath the light shined. (Isaiah 9:2, KJV)

Ah, for the privilege of standing before the archangels—the light of Uriel, the majesty of Gabriel, and triumph of Michael! We lesser angels look at them and tremble from afar. To be favored with a glance from them, to hear words pouring from their throats! Such encounters bless us and we are grateful for just that—their occasional attention to us.

Yet, Deep Heaven is filled with more activity than ever in this season, and even we, the lesser ones, know that the time of wonder is at hand. Gabriel has been very much in evidence, and he has favored us with many visits. I think he is looking us over. Some of us have been asked to sing in the great archangel's presence. He listens carefully and then departs. Where does he go? That is a question I would like to have answered.

Here he is now in full splendor. We are attentive before his presence. Gabriel stands so close to the Holy One that holiness surrounds him also and begins to blow toward us like a wind. We

breathe it in and are glad. He tells us the news that causes us
to bow—the One who has been with God from the beginning
is leaving Deep Heaven for the realm known as the earth. There
he will be born of a woman, to live the life of human beings.
The immortal one will become *anthropos*. If we had tears, we
would weep.

Gabriel announces that the time is at hand and that we who
are chosen will enter the human realm to sing the Son's praises at
his birth. I whisper, "If I were not so insignificant, I would beg to
be one of the heavenly choir," and immediately my name is called.
"You, the *insignificant* one," Gabriel says, "this is the spirit I am
looking for. Come and stand before me." I can barely move from
the awe and delight that have enveloped me. To enter the strange
realm of humanity, to see their lands, to sing in a language understood by them while praising the Holy One—what more can an
angel ever wish for?

The rest are gathered swiftly around as Gabriel instructs us.
There are many languages spoken on earth, he explains, but you will
choose one understood by shepherds, by the humble of the earth.

Glory to God in the highest, we sing, *hosanna in excelsis, doxa, doxa,
alleluiah.* We try words of praise in many languages until Gabriel is
satisfied that we will be understood by those who matter—the
humble and the clean of heart. "Learn to speak of peace on earth,"
he tells us. "Practice bringing news of God's good will to the people who are walking in darkness. They will see a great light, and
the light will come through you."

We, the lesser angels, are filled with joy, with song, with words
of goodness, as we are waiting for the wonder of God's breaking
forth into the human realm. If I had tears, I would weep.

Zechariah
The visitation

*"And you, child, will be called the prophet of the Most High;
for you will go before the Lord to prepare his ways. . . ."*
(Luke 1:76)

I remember standing before the altar enveloped by the smoke and smell of incense. I remember being glad that my lot had been drawn on that day when the division of Abijah, my ancestor, was on duty in God's Temple; I had entered the sanctuary, had offered the incense, but then, disillusioned and bored, I started counting and naming the other divisions in my head and, after I reached the eighth, mine, I was distracted and I no longer cared about my surroundings.

I was feeling old and tired. I was tasting disappointment and bitterness together with the smell of incense that was entering my throat. I was wishing that I would become drunk on it. I, Zechariah, of the division of Abijah, I who had lived a righteous life with a good wife from the house of Aaron, had not been blessed with a child. *Soon I will be dead, and no one will remember me,* I thought, and great sadness filled me. Everyone else was outside, praying. No one could see me.

And it was then that the unthinkable happened to one who was not occupied with holy thoughts but with bitter ones. He appeared at the right side of the altar and I recognized him immediately—

an angel of the Lord whose countenance made me tremble. I knew I would die. I prayed I would die. Maybe this is why his first words were: "Do not be afraid, Zechariah." He knew my name, of course. I immediately took courage and dared to lift my eyes to see the brightness of him, but his words continued, and I found myself laughing uncontrollably. I had been dreaming of a child and there was Gabriel, who stands in the presence of God, promising me one. Tears were running from my eyes and he must have thought they were from laughter, but they were from terror. He was promising me gladness, he was promising me joy, but only later did I remember his words. At that moment of terror and disbelief, I focused on only one astounding promise: "even before his birth he will be filled with the Holy Spirit."

I dared to open my mouth. "How will I know?" I asked. I wanted proof. I reminded him that both I and Elizabeth were now old, beyond child-producing, child-bearing years. As if he didn't know.

Was there a smile on Gabriel's face? How can one tell on such a fierce and holy countenance? But I have this feeling that he was thinking, *You want a sign, I will give you a sign.* And he did.

After he had gone, I moved like a drunk to the exit. It was time for me to bless the people. I lifted my arms, I opened my mouth, but nothing came out. They started mumbling and nudging each other. I motioned to them to be quiet. I pointed to the sky, and then I pointed inside in the direction of the altar, and suddenly I was filled with joy unspeakable. This was the sign; this was the beginning of the fulfillment of the promise. The child would come.

The people, now convinced that I had seen a vision, left reluctantly and I was alone to praise God with my mind if not my voice. I fulfilled the rest of my time as serving priest with meticulous attention but I could hardly find the necessary patience to keep me from rushing home to Elizabeth.

A few days later we returned to our home in the hill country west of Jerusalem. The joy we felt at the coming of the child was countered only by Elizabeth's amazement at finding herself preg-

nant at an age when she should be tending grandchildren. Instead
of embarrassment, she felt such joy that she could not contain it
among others—they would think her arrogant—so she chose to
stay inside our home, to prepare for the baby's coming. My deep
silence was invaded by her constant singing.

She had entered her sixth month when a visitor arrived from
Nazareth, her lovely young cousin Mariam. At that moment
Elizabeth was transformed. She ran out of the house and the two
of them broke into song. I should have been surprised, but I was not.
After the visit of Gabriel nothing surprised me. It was Mariam's
visit that caused me to remember the words the blessed Gabriel
had uttered, and it was she who taught me their meaning: "to
make ready a people prepared for the Lord."

When Elizabeth first greeted Mariam and the child in her
womb danced his joy, I understood the words of Gabriel, that
"even before his birth he will be filled with the Holy Spirit."

When evening fell and we sat together with Mariam to hear
her story, I felt a deep assurance that the time of the Messiah had
come and that Mariam was carrying him. She told us of the
blessed Gabriel's words to her, of Joseph's fears, and of her own
mother's anxiety. And we, in turn, offered her comfort, protection
from prying eyes, and our conviction that she was blessed by the
Holy One. When she left three months later, some of the light left
with her, but immediately we made ready for John's arrival, and
nothing in life was the same for us afterward. The words that came
from my newly opened mouth and my exuberant voice convinced
me of God's new creation:

> By the tender mercy of our God,
> the dawn from on high will break upon us,
> to give light to those who sit in darkness and in the
> shadow of death,
> to guide our feet into the way of peace.

Blessed be God's Holy Name.

Elizabeth and Mariam
In the hill country

Now the time came for Elizabeth to give birth, and she bore a son. Her neighbors and relatives heard that the Lord had shown his great mercy to her, and they rejoiced with her. (Luke 1:57–58)

There was a man sent from God, whose name was John. He came as a witness to testify to the light, so that all might believe through him. He himself was not the light, but he came to testify to the light. The true light, which enlightens everyone, was coming into the world. (John 1:6–9)

Mariam's visit filled me with words I hadn't known. That time of wonders and angel-song was full of light, but it was the words that surprised me. When I saw my lovely young cousin coming uphill and I recognized her, I left the seclusion of my home to meet her. And my baby danced inside me. Then I knew. The recognition was unmistakable—one baby to the other: Welcome!

In our part of the world it is the young who respect the old. But there I was, a woman with gray in the hair, a large baby in my belly, bending down to praise Mariam, who was young enough to be my daughter. "Why has this happened to me, that the mother of my Lord comes to me?" I kept asking her. And she, so young and innocent, accepted the title without question.

Something was happening inside us—were the babies in our wombs conversing? I am too ignorant to understand these things, but we both knew that the words we uttered were not ours. Zechariah calls all this the work of the Holy Spirit, and he, a priest, ought to know. But what I do know is my body, and it was responding to the life being formed in Mariam. For, on that first day, the girl became a prophet—it is the only way I can understand it. A pious girl, she knew her Scriptures and the poems of old, but I did not think it was Samuel's mother Hannah she was remembering: the words were her own. The God who for so long seemed to belong only to the men of Israel was suddenly ours also, in a most intimate, wondrous way. And Mariam understood the heart of our God with a clarity that stuns me still, after these many years of joy and immense sorrow. "Surely, from now on all generations will call me blessed," she sang, and I did not doubt it. And when I told her of my shame all these years, of the blame I received because I was barren, she said, "Elizabeth, rejoice, for God 'has lifted up the lowly.'"

"Yes," I said. "Yes, I have been lifted up."

And on our walks, as she looked at the fields becoming gold for the harvest, she cried out, "He has filled the hungry with good things, and sent the rich away empty."

Zechariah couldn't talk ever since he had heard the announcement of our baby's coming, but he listened, smiled, and nodded. I am gifted with the needle, so I helped Mariam prepare the baby clothes. What did we talk about?

She recounted Joseph's fears and her concern for him as she told him of her baby's coming. She wept when she described his goodness in saving her life, and his willingness to obey the Lord as she herself had done. She talked of her mother and father and their worries for her safety. The cruelty of our laws toward women who have babies out of wedlock is legendary. Joseph's quick decision to marry her saved her life, she said. And in all this, she gave God the thanks and glory.

One day we were alone together, and I took her hands in mine and said, "Mariam, my dear, our sons will not have an easy life. It is a terrible burden to be God's chosen."

Her eyes filled with tears as she said, "I know. From the moment Gabriel appeared to me, I have known."

"And I have another conviction," I continued, sure of this now. "My son will prepare the way for yours."

"But how?" she asked. "Why?"

"This is God's will," I answered. "This is what Zechariah wrote on a tablet yesterday—the words of Gabriel to him. He had forgotten them until he saw you. Listen: 'He will turn many of the people of Israel to the Lord their God. With the spirit and power of Elijah he will go before him, to turn the hearts of parents to their children, and the disobedient to the wisdom of the righteous, to make ready a people prepared for the Lord.'"

Mariam said, "I don't understand now, but one day I will." And then she changed the direction of the conversation and all her youth came to the fore. "Elizabeth, you are preparing lovely little shifts for my son, but I see nothing as fine for yours," and I almost wept. I had not told her the rest of Zechariah's message.

"He is to be a Nazirite, Mariam. This one," and I patted my belly, "this one will live in the wilderness and will not drink wine nor will he cut his hair."

She put her arms around me. "Oh, if only we could have the assurance that they will belong to us!" she said, for we both knew that John and Yeshua would belong to the world. We mothers would have them only for a little while. But for that, we were grateful. "My soul magnifies the Lord, and my spirit rejoices in God my Savior," she sang, and I joined in.

Joseph
A visit from Mariam
and the angel Gabriel

Her husband Joseph, being a righteous man and unwilling to expose her to public disgrace, planned to dismiss her quietly. (Matthew 1:19)

When Joseph awoke from sleep, he did as the angel of the Lord commanded him; he took her as his wife, but had no marital relations with her until she had borne a son; and he named him Jesus. (Matthew 1:24–25)

How foolish are the plans of men! When I chose Mariam as my betrothed, all I wanted was an ordinary life in Nazareth. What I received has shaken my foundations. I remember that day and I still cringe inside.

She stood on the threshold of my workshop and I stared at her, unable to utter a word. Her sweet voice spoke the words, and her face remained serene, but her eyes were troubled. "Joseph, my dear, my betrothed, my good friend. I must tell you this myself before you hear it from my parents. I am with child, Joseph. And I have no idea how it happened." My immediate reaction was to smash something, but only her face was before me, and how could I hurt Mariam?

We are not given to jokes in our village. Life is hard, and we take it seriously. But for a wild, hopeful moment, I thought she was being funny. I waited for her to explain. She gave me one of her radiant smiles, but her eyes were filled with tears. "The only thing about this wondrous event, the only thing that saddens me is that you are hurt, Joseph."

Hurt? She couldn't begin to guess what anger choked me, what bile filled my mouth. I stared at her, and then, afraid of what I might do, I motioned for her to go away. She obeyed. And there I sat for hours, in the workshop that smelled of the familiar wood chips, tasting my bitterness, unable to move. A man of action up to now, I felt paralyzed. My head was too heavy for my neck. I placed my elbows on my knees and rested my throbbing forehead in my hands. "God of my ancestors," I cried. "How can I shame her before the world? Help me, show me what I must do." And I felt the tears burning my eyes, bringing some relief from the anger.

From the moment she told me the fearful news I knew that I should wait. I must not act hastily, I told myself. I must not shame her. But what galled me was that she was *not* ashamed when she told me. Shame seemed the farthest thing from her mind. Why? Why?

The only opening in my workshop was the door, so even with my head bowed, I knew that by the time I stopped crying out to God the light in the room had changed. It was more than that: this light had a sound—it wavered between a song and lighted speech. I raised my head and looked directly into the sun. How was it possible? Up here in Nazareth, the sun should be heading for the western hills at this hour, not entering my hut full force.

The brilliant light, however, didn't burn my eyes; it started taking shape. So, trembling from head to toe, I asked, "Who are you?" I had no evidence, but I was certain this was a person. I knew I was in the presence of someone.

"I am God's messenger." The meaning entered my head clearly though I could not distinguish words. "For the sake of men like you, Joseph, son of David, I am called by the name Gabriel."

I fell on my knees then. God's angel had come to visit *me*? I felt my whole body shaking. The voice said, "Do not be afraid," and my trembling ceased. "Now that you are no longer afraid of me," Gabriel continued, "you need to lose the other fear that caused you to cry out to God. God has heard you, Joseph, and the message is this: Do not be afraid to take Mariam as your wife."

I lifted my head to speak but the angel made a movement that hushed me. "I know, Joseph. I know she is with child. This is why you must not be afraid. Oh, if you only knew! This child is a gift of the Holy Spirit, so you will accept Mariam as your wife and honor her. When the child is born, you will be there, Joseph, and you will name him Jesus, for he is destined to save his people."

I waited, and the angel seemed to be waiting also. A great peace enveloped me as my heart filled with love for Mariam and for the child in her womb. I stood up. "I will do as you have said," I said to the angel, but when I looked again, he was no longer there. I wanted to rush to Mariam, but I stood still for a long while savoring what I had heard. I did not know whether I had been awake or asleep when the angel appeared, but now I was fully awake.

I had so many questions, but they no longer mattered. It was as if Gabriel had answered them all, only I had not yet discovered the answers. They would come slowly, like apparitions in the night. Life would not be ordinary, but I was now filled with the assurance that I could handle it. "Someone is with me," I said aloud to the familiar room that still glowed with the light of the visitor. "I don't have to face this alone."

I left my workshop to go to her, to tell her, but when I was still some distance from her house, Mariam, laughing, ran out to meet me.

Anna

The news my daughter brought me

The virgin's name was Mary. And [the angel] came to her and said, "Greetings, favored one! The Lord is with you." But she was much perplexed by his words and pondered what sort of greeting this might be. (Luke 1:27–29)

Then Mary said, "Here am I, the servant of the Lord; let it be with me according to your word." (Luke 1:38)

I brought her up to be good. Life was hard for all of us. Having enough to eat was a daily worry, but her father and I knew that she was the one who mattered, and we did without so she could grow up to be healthy and strong. The merciful God gave us only this one child, and we thanked the Creator by teaching our daughter to honor God's Holy Name.

This is what we did: We told her the stories of God's blessings on our people, we prayed daily, and we observed the Law.

Mariam was a good girl. She was pious and gentle, obedient to us, and observant of the Law of Moses. What more could parents want of their daughter? Before her birth, we had promised her to Joseph of the house of David, and when he was old enough to do so he chose her for himself. My line was from the same house and Joachim's was from the Levitic line. We knew it was a good match. Joseph was a young boy running around when

Mariam was born. They grew up knowing that they belonged together. When she was of age, the betrothal was announced and we were content. "If we die early," Joachim said, "Joseph will care for our child." What more could a parent wish for a daughter?

It was a few months before the wedding. On the appointed day, Joseph would come to lead her to his home and we would no longer have her near us day and night, but she would still be in Nazareth and I would watch my grandchildren grow. I thanked God for the mercy poured on us, though I knew I would miss her sweet voice intoning the prayers and singing the psalms. What a comfort the girl was. When someone asked me those days what was her most noticeable quality, I would say—obedience.

This is why the news came as such a shock, such a bitter disappointment. We don't always notice our children, do we? Day in, day out, we live with their joyful presence and don't pay attention to the changes. But something had been different about her the last few weeks. There was a glow on her face, more so than usual, and I thought, *She is looking forward to the wedding.* When we shared our meal of the day, she was unusually quiet and, every now and then, I saw a puzzled expression on her face—at times a serious concern, other times, a kind of wonder. "She is a little bit worried about leaving us," I whispered to Joachim one night. "Being an only child puts a burden on her." Joachim patted my hand. "We will miss her," he agreed. "But soon her place will be with Joseph. This is as God willed it." I nodded, but kept looking at her secretly when she withdrew into her world of puzzlement and wonder.

So when she sought me out one morning, I was not too surprised. I was waiting for her to ask me the questions that girls who are about to be married need answered. She kissed my hand, and then she raised her eyes to me, and I saw they were filled with tears.

"What is the matter, my child?" I asked. "Are you frightened?"

She said, "No, no. I am only frightened for you, my mother."

"For me? But why, Mariam? I am happy for you. I have known Joseph since he was born. He is a good man."

"Oh, my mother, I do know this better than anyone. He is a good man indeed. You and Father chose well for me. What I am about to tell you will upset you, but you must listen to me before you speak. Promise, will you promise?"

I started feeling something akin to fear. What was the child trying to tell me? I nodded and tried to pull her down close to me. "No, Mother," she said. "I must remain standing. I may have to run, to hide, after I tell you."

Now I was really worried. I remembered with a chill that she had not withdrawn when her monthly time came but continued to work alongside me. I caught my breath. "Mariam, you have not been with Joseph, have you?"

She understood immediately. "No, Mother, of course not. I wish it were that simple."

"Simple? Has someone hurt you? Has someone defiled you?"

At that she laughed, and I felt a bit of relief. "What is it, then? What is it?"

Her eyes spilled the tears but a strange light shone on her face. I almost closed my own eyes. I was now trembling as if a chill had come over me, though it was very hot outside.

"How can I speak of what cannot be put into words?" she said, as if talking to herself.

"Everything can be put into words," I said, now getting a little annoyed, ready to admonish her.

She shook her head. "Not the appearance of an angel," she said. "How can I describe it?"

"An angel?" I whispered, and the awe descended upon me.

She noticed. "Yes," she agreed in the same hushed tone. "This is what it feels like—the fear of the Lord."

I waited. All desire to admonish her had left me. I waited for her to find the words because what I felt was new—a fear mixed with wonder. Yes, she was right—this is what our ancestors called the fear of the Lord.

"One day as I was praying alone," she started, and I saw how her face shone, and I almost knelt before my child. "On that day the angel Gabriel appeared before me to bring me the good news. . . ."

She was lost again in the memory. "The good news?" I urged her. "What good news?"

She looked faraway and now she was quoting: "Be joyful, most grace-filled maiden! The Lord is with you."

I cried aloud and that brought her back to me. "These are the words I heard, Mother. Listen." She closed her eyes and she intoned: "'Do not be afraid, Mariam, for you have found favor with God. And now, you will conceive in your womb and bear a son, and you will name him Jesus. . . .'" She opened her eyes. "There was more," she said, "but that can wait."

"What did you say?" I asked fearing the answer but knowing it.

"I asked immediately, 'How can this happen? I have not been with a man.'"

She was quiet again, lost in thought and memory. "How can this be?" I repeated her question. "What did the blessed Gabriel say?"

"I think he laughed. 'Nothing will be impossible with God,' he assured me, and then he explained: 'The Holy Spirit will come upon you, and the power of the Most High will overshadow you; therefore the child to be born will be holy; he will be called Son of God.'"

I reached out and held my child. After a while I asked her, "What did you say?"

"I answered, 'Here am I, the servant of the Lord; let it be with me according your word.' I think that satisfied him. When I looked up, he was gone."

We held each other and wept for a long time. Then I said, "I must tell Joseph."

But Mariam was firm with me. "No, my mother, I will go to Joseph. He deserves to hear this from me."

And she left while I stayed home on my knees, praying for them both.

Joachim
A father's shock and recognition

*Honor your father and your mother, as the LORD your God
commanded you, so that your days may be long and that it may
go well with you in the land that the LORD your God is giving you.* (Deuteronomy 5:16)

*"Go, lie down; and if he calls you, you shall say, 'Speak, LORD,
for your servant is listening.'"* (1 Samuel 3:9)

"It is the LORD; let him do what seems good to him." (1 Samuel
3:18b)

I said to Anna, "Other fathers would send her away never to return,
never to speak to her again. She shamed our family. Think about
what you are asking me to do." And Anna wept and wept. "I
thought you were different from other husbands, other fathers," she
told me, and I guessed at that moment that wives must have been
saying those words to their husbands from the beginning of time.

"Why should I be different?" I asked my wife. She had been
a good wife, so I knew that I should pay attention, not dismiss her.
"Tell me, why should I be different from those fathers who have
obeyed the Law at times like these?"

"Because you know our daughter," was her answer, as if that
made all the difference. "Think," she continued. "Remember. Has

there ever been any time when this child of ours did anything we considered bad before God's eyes? Has there ever been any event in her young life that worried us or brought shame to our name? Has she ever disobeyed you, her father?"

Anger at the news had kept me from thinking, from remembering. But now my wife was asking me some serious questions, and I owed her thoughtful answers. She was not one to nag or to speak out of turn. She was not a woman given to gossip or to thinking ill of her neighbors. Anna was a good woman who kept our home pious before the Lord with her prayers and her wise counsel. So for a moment I felt ashamed that I had lashed out at her and at Mariam without giving them a chance to explain. Mariam had left the room in tears but Anna stood up to me and faced me.

I said, "No, she has not disobeyed me and has not displeased me. But this one act of hers does away with all the years of obedience. This is the worst that can happen to a father."

"Is it worse than what is happening to her?" Anna asked me, and I heard in her voice the fervor for justice that I had admired in her when she was defending others. "This is our daughter," my wife continued, her passion making her voice tremble, "our good, beloved daughter. I believe her when she says she has not been with a man. Why don't you?"

"Because I know men, and I know the weakness of women," I answered without thinking.

My wife held her ground. "Oh, you do? What women are you talking about, Joachim? How many weak women have you known? Your own mother, your wife, your daughter? Tell me which one of us weaklings you have in mind." At that moment, I heard her, really heard what she was asking me and I thought, *Man, she has you there. What a silly thing for you to say. She is right, of course.* I didn't answer her, but she was not so easily put off. "I am waiting," she insisted. "Tell me about the weakness of women."

"I spoke without thinking," I admitted, so that she would stop staring at me with those probing eyes. This mild-mannered woman had all of a sudden become fierce. Daring to doubt our daughter had done for her what all the trials of our past life had not achieved. I was astounded. She deserved to be treated as I would have treated a man I trusted and knew well.

"Listen, Anna. I want to believe you and Mariam. But you must admit that women don't find themselves with child out of thin air, do they? What do you expect me to think?"

"I expect you to give your daughter the same trust that I gave her. Do you think it was an easy thing for me to hear? But she has never given me cause to doubt her and she has never given you cause to doubt her. So why don't you listen? If she had been a son, would you have listened?"

Where has this woman been hiding? I asked myself. I was shaken. I was weakening. "Let me go away to pray to the Almighty," I said, and walked outside toward the hill that was behind the house. I walked quickly, thinking hard, and asking God the Merciful to give me some light and some hope that this disaster would pass from me. As I walked with my head hanging down, praying without sound in a hopelessness that told me my prayers were going nowhere, I had a glimpse of someone else farther away, kneeling by a rock. With a start I recognized my daughter Mariam, who seemed to be lost in prayer. I looked at her with something like envy because there was no question from her posture and her face that her prayers were being heard and were being answered. I turned around and returned to my wife.

"Forgive me, wife," I said. "Do you think Mariam will find it in her heart to forgive me?"

The good woman put her arms around me. "It is not forgiveness that is being asked of us," she said, "but something even more difficult. What is being asked of us is to trust and to wait—to wait in faith, as Mariam is doing, for the child that is to come."

Mariam's Childhood Friend
Sharing secrets in Nazareth

In those days Mary set out and went with haste to a Judean town in the hill country.... (Luke 1:39)

And Mary remained with [Elizabeth] for about three months and then returned to her home. (Luke 1:56)

Then his mother and his brothers came; and standing outside, they sent to him and called him. A crowd was sitting around him; and they said to him, "Your mother and your brothers and sisters are outside, asking for you." And he replied, "Who are my mother and my brothers?" (Mark 3:31–33)

She was my best and dearest friend. We were born in the same month, in the village of Nazareth, and my parents had known Joachim and Anna since their childhood days also. Descendants of David or descendants of a peasant, we were all the same. Our fathers tilled the soil and our mothers wove the cloth for the clothes we wore. We ate one meal a day and drank the good water of Nazareth. We were strong children used to running up and down the hills of the village. Mariam and I didn't have any secrets because we told each other everything.

One day, when we had nothing to do and were sitting on the rocks thinking in silence, the way girls do, I looked at her and watched her face closely as I revealed my desire to stay single, not to marry. Now, had I confessed this to anyone else, the reaction would have been one of near horror. But Mariam heard me out, then leaned her chin on her palm pensively and remained in deep thought 'for quite a while. I was comfortable with this because I knew that she took her time in answering questions. It was one of the many qualities I liked in her. Finally, she said: "It's a strange desire for a girl our age. Our Hebrew ways don't encourage celibacy in women. Can you tell me why it is that you don't want to marry?"

"It's because I want to fight," I told her, and at that she lost her calm and looked very surprised indeed. "I want to join a group that will defeat the Romans," I added, and it is to her credit that she did not laugh at me.

"I don't think they allow women to fight," she said seriously. "It would be very difficult to find any men who would be willing to accept you as one of them, one of their group."

"I plan to disguise myself as a man," I retorted, and at that she smiled and looked me up and down. "Now you tell me about *your* dream, your desire," I asked her.

"I want to be obedient to God and to do God's will," she answered immediately, as if she had given it a great deal of thought already.

And I said, just to be obstinate, "Wouldn't it be marvelous if *I* could fight and *you* could be a rabbi?" We both laughed aloud at that, but then we grew thoughtful and sad because we knew that such dreams were not the lot of women.

I'm recalling all this so that you will see how unjust I was to her when her miracle happened. I had started noticing a strange light about her—her eyes, her mouth, the way she would fall silent and stand still for long minutes, the sudden tears that glistened in her eyes—and I wondered if she had fallen in love, something not encouraged in our village where marriages were arranged. So I asked her outright and she smiled—a rather sad smile, I thought at the time.

"No, no," she answered. "Of course, I do love Joseph. He's such a good man, and we have known each other for years. This is not about Joseph, though I am worried about him; it's something else, but I find it very difficult to tell you."

"But I'm your very best friend," I cried. "How can you keep anything from me?"

She took my hands in hers and looked at me as if reading me. "I know, I know. Yet, even you will find this very hard to take," she said in preparation for the shocking news. "You are my friend, indeed, and it cannot be kept secret for long, so I should tell you now." I waited, even though I was about to burst with curiosity.

"I am with child," she said very quietly and I screamed, as girls do.

"Well, then, you should marry Joseph right away," I managed to say when I stopped squealing, but at that she shook her head.

"If I tell you it is not Joseph's child, what will you say?" she asked, and it was at that moment I betrayed her. I turned my back and walked away from my best friend, I who had wanted to break all the rules and go fight with men. She didn't call after me; she let me go.

Later, when I thought about it, I wondered why I had reacted with such stubbornness. Mariam had been such a good girl, so pious and serious and obedient to her parents, that her news was not easy to accept. But I was her friend; I should have listened. So a few days later, repentant, I went to find her, but her mother told me that Mariam had left for her cousin's home in Judea.

I had not spoken to anyone about Mariam's news, but I found myself abandoned and guilty at having betrayed my best friend's confidence by walking away from her. Anna, her mother, saw my distress and invited me to stay a while. "I am lonely without Mariam," she said and looked at me very carefully, as older women do when they know something. So I burst it out. "Why did she leave without telling me?"

"What did you do when she gave you her news?" Anna asked me instead of answering.

"So you too know about her," I whispered to her mother.

"She told me immediately," Anna said. "My first reaction was one of disbelief also."

"But how could this happen, when Mariam goes nowhere without your knowing. . . ," and like a fool I burst into tears. "She's my best friend," I blubbered. "How could she do this to me?" Her good mother didn't laugh at me for that ridiculous question.

She waited until I pulled myself together and then she said, "There are things, my child, we do not understand and never will. I believe this is one of them. We cannot point to anyone who fathered Mariam's child, for the word came to her from the angel Gabriel."

"That's what comes from spending so many hours listening to the prophets and thinking about their words," I said without thinking, and her mother managed a laugh at that absurd statement. We sat together and talked for a long time and she tried to share with me what Mariam had told her. Since then I have been wondering, *Who is the Holy Spirit?*

I can hardly wait for my friend's return so I can tell her how sorry I am. If I were to pretend that I understand what has happened to her I would not be telling the truth. I still don't know who the Holy Spirit is, what the angel Gabriel looks like, why Mariam was chosen for something so extraordinary and frightening. Her mother said to me: "There are some things we don't understand, but when love is present, we can accept them and love the ones who are chosen by God, no matter how great the cost to them." That's all I know.

Should I feel sorry for Mariam? Should I rejoice for her? Together with her mother, I am waiting for my friend.

A Barren Woman
Waiting in Bethlehem,
in ordinary time

"Blessed are the barren, and the wombs that never bore, and the breasts that never nursed." (Luke 23:29b)

I believe that I shall see the goodness of the LORD in the land of the living. (Psalm 27:13)

I want to tell you what my life was like in Bethlehem that year when Augustus was still emperor and Herod was triumphant in Jerusalem. Someone once told me that Jerusalem was only ten kilometers away, but for me it was in another world. We only *heard* of Herod's riches and excesses; we never saw them. Here, in Bethlehem, we lived in poverty and barely survived.

It was a small village, though a man who knew how to read told me it was all-important because it was named by the prophets. We were of Jesse's tree, he said. The great king, David, was from Bethlehem and that was enough glory for all of us. But does this fill our bellies? I asked, and knew the answer. I used to wonder—why does it matter where people are born? But it does, doesn't it? What would my life have been like had I been born in Jerusalem instead of Bethlehem? I would have married someone else; it's even possible that I could have been wealthy, not having to work every one of my waking hours. Now *that* would have been different.

Or—my life would not have been quite so sad. I'm trying to avoid telling you this part, but my story won't make sense to you unless you know my sorrow. When I was young, in my father's house, I used to think, *When I marry, things will be different. I will be in my husband's home and I'll have my own children to love.*

A good man did marry me, but every child I conceived in my womb died shortly after being born. Time after time I felt the joy of life beginning in me only to have it snuffed out. I wanted to join my little children. I wanted to die, but that was not in my hands. Yet, never seeing what I anticipated with so much joy live to find fulfillment was a fate worse than death. What kind of god was doing this to me?

I became so despondent that my husband borrowed every shekel he could to send me away from Bethlehem, to forget my sorrows. He offered to take me to Jerusalem, but all I wanted was to disappear in the countryside, to be alone among the hills. I started walking, not knowing where I was going. The countryside was bare; the hills looked scorched. But every now and then I would come upon a village and there I would rest and listen to the talk of the people in the square. And every now and then I would find an orchard of figs and olives, and just the sight of them would refresh me.

One day I came upon two women walking together in a field, absorbed in conversation. It was in the hill country of Judea, west of Bethlehem. The wheat was growing tall and only their heads seemed to float above the stalks. They were so well hidden that I did not notice that one of them was great with child until I was directly in front of them. What I saw surprised me. One was young and in the bloom of health, probably just beginning to feel life growing in her womb, but the other, much older, was showing, and her baby would be coming soon. I was so shocked that I stopped and stared.

They broke off speaking when they saw me but approached me without curiosity, just concerned to see me so upset. "Do not be afraid," the young woman said.

"I'm not afraid," I said to her, and then I burst into loud weeping and did not know how to stop. They stood by, waiting for me to collect myself. I cried it out to the older one: "It's so unfair that you—already old enough to have grandchildren—you are with child, and I am not!"

The woman didn't even seem perturbed. "Yes, it is," she agreed. "This is the reason I have hidden myself for so long, but now the baby is coming, and there is not much I can do about it but rejoice."

I was so grateful for her understanding that I told them about all my failed pregnancies and the dead infants. "Come," the older one said, "come home with us, and we will tell you our stories. I am Elizabeth, and this is my cousin Mariam." She added as we walked to her house, "Mariam is ready to return home to Nazareth, and we were spending a last blissful morning together."

I was sorry then about intruding on their friendship but I didn't have the heart to leave them. Their presence was like a balm to my wounded heart. Elizabeth told me of waiting for years and years for her child, bearing the shame, hearing all her neighbors blame her childlessness on herself. "When I had given up hope," she told me, "God answered my prayers."

When Mariam's turn came she recounted her utter surprise when she found herself with child. "Unlike you two, I had not asked for him," she said. "Why I was chosen only God knows, but I cannot question God."

I knew I was in the presence of two holy women who had every right to look down on me and my problems, but they did not. "Why are women always blamed for childlessness?" Elizabeth wondered aloud, but we had no answer.

"Not only women," Mariam added with a sad smile, "but also God." I felt that she was reading my mind. She continued, "The only assurance I have is that God has done great things for me, for us, and holy is his name. His mercy is on those who fear him throughout all generations."

I believed her. Why? I cannot know, but I did. I returned home, magnifying the Lord our God as Mariam had done, following her example. I now live with the hope that I will see those two little ones my new friends are expecting grow up to serve their Lord. Their mothers will see to it. For the first time, I am content to be waiting also, trusting in God's goodness.

Mariam

The Virgin contemplates
the words of her song

Then Mary said, "Here am I, the servant of the Lord; let it be with me according to your word." (Luke 1:38)

"Surely, from now on all generations will call me blessed. . . ." (Luke 1:48)

And Mary remained with [Elizabeth] for about three months and then returned to her home." (Luke 1:56)

I have left Elizabeth and Zechariah's to return home to my parents and to Joseph. As I walk in the early morning light, I think about the three months we spent together, the peace and welcome I found in my cousin's home, the reassurance that all would be well because it is God's hand that is supporting and guiding us.

During my days with them I did not think much about the astounding welcome I received from Elizabeth on my arrival, nor of the words that poured forth from my mouth as if someone else were speaking in my stead. But now, on these long hours of walking until I meet with the caravan that is traveling to Nazareth, I cannot get them out of my mind. What was it that I felt when Elizabeth knelt and called me "the mother of my Lord"? Why didn't I stop her? Why did I respond to her with words I had not known, I had not thought up on my own?

As I trudge along, conscious now of the growing life within me, I sing them in my mind and I tremble. Was I being proud? And isn't this the sin we have been warned against committing?

My soul magnifies the Lord, and my spirit rejoices in God my Savior.

Yes, this is what my heart sings. This is what I want always to remember and to hold on to. This is good. Don't forget this joy.

For the Mighty One has done great things for me, and holy is his name.

Oh, yes, holy is his name. But what is this great thing God has done for me? Am I only wishing that it will happen? I must examine it. I do give thanks to God for this life within me. But will I still sing this song if something happens to my child? What if he dies young? What if his life is filled with sorrow? Elizabeth's words stay with me: *What a burden on those who give birth to God's chosen.* How can I bear it? Ah, all mothers must have these fears; take them away from me, Holy One. God of my father and my mother, give me the grace to accept your gift, no matter what befalls me. Let all sorrow come to me but not to him.

His mercy is for those who fear him from generation to generation.

This is the easiest part. My good parents have taught me about the fear of the Lord, the awe and trembling in the presence of holiness, and we have been assured of God's mercy all our lives. I accept it with gratitude.

He has brought down the powerful from their thrones, and lifted up the lowly.

I stop to rest, sit under a tree, and contemplate these words. Why did they come to me? What do they mean? Is it possible that this Babe in my body will have something to do with the powerful and those who sit on thrones? Oh God of Abraham, no! This, this is what frightens me. If he interferes with the powerful, they will seek to destroy him.

I close my eyes to make the fear go away, but instead I see Gabriel's fiery form before me. *"You have found favor with God, Mariam, and the child to be born will be great, and will be called the Son of the Most High, and the Lord God will give to him the throne of his ancestor David. . . ."* I was so stunned when he spoke that I could not follow much of what he said after that. But when I asked him—when I reminded him that I had been with no man—he said the words that I would struggle to explain to Joseph, to my mother, even to Elizabeth: *"The child to be born will be holy; he will be called Son of God."*

What does this mean? I wonder. The words about David and thrones confuse me. My child cannot possibly become a king like David. Look at me. I am a peasant, no matter what my ancestry. And if he is to be king, why did the Lord put the words in my mouth about this child's future, about bringing down the powerful from their thrones? Aren't kings powerful?

Did I truly hear the words of Gabriel? Did I dream them or wish them because I long—we *all* long—for Messiah, the anointed one who is to bring liberation from the pagan oppressors of our land? Help me to know your truth, O Lord!

I stand up, the questions troubling my mind, but my heart is at peace. I am in God's hands—this I know.

He has shown strength with his arm; he has scattered the proud in the thoughts of their hearts.

I look down below at the road I will be joining soon. The people are walking north together, bent under their burdens. A few Roman soldiers pass, proud and tall on their horses. They look at the poor crowd and laugh. I feel tears sting my eyes and I pat the baby in my body. "Come, Holy One," I pray, and then I hear the words that have been singing themselves in my mind:

He has brought down the powerful from their thrones, and lifted up the lowly; he has filled the hungry with good things, and the rich he has sent away empty.

Yes, I am ready. Come, Holy One.

A Midwife
Journeying to Bethlehem
with a swallow for company

For now the winter is past,
the rain is over and gone.
The flowers appear on the earth;
the time of singing has come,
and the voice of the turtledove
is heard in our land. (Song of Solomon 2:11–12)

A swallow kept flying overhead throughout the long journey. I wondered why it was attracted to that particular woman in a manner that made it appear solicitous. *Is it possible,* I thought at first, *that there is a nest somewhere in the couple's belongings, maybe under that basket hanging down the donkey's left side?* She seemed concerned not to tire the donkey. She was quite heavy with child but when I looked at her face I saw how young she was and I decided I should look after her. Her mother was not with her, but her husband was very attentive, almost unable to take his eyes off her. He looked at her as if she were precious beyond all worldly treasure. Still, he was a man and men don't know about such things as birthing babies.

"You must be newlyweds," I said to her on the second day, a foolish statement under the obvious circumstances, but she smiled up at him and her face was radiant. "I have known him all my life," she said simply. He looked at me very carefully as if trying to determine my worthiness but remained quiet.

The young mother-to-be looked in excellent health, but I had had both children and grandchildren and knew how difficult it was to travel long distances in her condition, so I offered my services in the event the baby came early. I had been a midwife in the court of Herod, but one of his wives, in a fit of temper, had dismissed me. I looked at the young couple again and compared them in my mind to the sons and daughters of Herod. I shook my head. At that moment the swallow swooped close to her and the girl laughed aloud. She told me her name was Mariam and her husband was Joseph. They were from Nazareth. I had joined the caravan south of the town, close to the Sea of Galilee. They were returning to Bethlehem and I to Jerusalem, heading to our respective birthplaces for the census.

The swallow hovered overhead and Mariam lifted her eyes to it, then turned to Joseph as if asking him a question. But he only smiled. "Is this a bird from your home, daughter?" I asked her, but I knew that people didn't train swallows, not the way doves and pigeons could be trained. "It seems to be following only you, no one else."

She looked up again and shook her head. "I don't remember seeing it at home," she answered, "but I welcome it on this long journey. It may be following this good servant of humanity, the kind donkey." At that moment a sound from the donkey that sounded more like a snicker than anything else interrupted us and we both laughed, though my laugh was forced. *What is going on here? Are these people magicians who can talk to animals?* I wondered.

We lapsed into quiet; it was getting toward twilight and soon we would be making preparations for the night's rest. There were very few inns along the way and most of the caravan stayed close together under the stars or with a stretched cloth overhead to keep us from feeling the night dew. The sun was setting, but in the sweet light of evening a quiet fell on the group and the swallow flew one last circle overhead, then lowered its graceful self and perched on top of the donkey's head and sat there as if protecting the little family, a kind of lookout.

Mariam turned and said something to her husband in a soft voice, but I was close enough to hear and felt the hairs prickling on my skin. "It may be the Holy Spirit looking after the child," she said, "making sure nothing happens to him." And she laughed uncertainly, as if not quite believing what she said. But he looked at the bird and his face was very serious. He said to her, "Ah, Mariam, these days nothing surprises me, but I am glad for every sign of protection for you and the little one. May the Holy One be praised."

Their words went through my ears into my head and sat there waiting to be examined. I looked at the bird that appeared black as it sat in repose, its scissor-like tail folded so the silver didn't show through, and I tried to remember references to birds as spirits. *Who is the Holy Spirit?* I wanted to know, but this time I was hesitant to ask. I approached the husband and said, "Young man, I am a trained midwife. If you need me in the night, you must not hesitate to call on me. I will rest nearby."

He turned then and really looked at me. "It is an offer I honor," he told me in his rather formal manner. "I know the Lord is protecting Mariam, but I will be glad for any help with the birthing." Mariam turned and smiled her radiant smile at me. "My mother would be so comforted to know that you are here."

In the morning I looked around for the bird but it had flown away. As soon as the animals were summoned and the burdens put upon them, we were ready to resume the journey. I wondered how Mariam had slept. "The donkey offered me his strong side," she said, "and I leaned on it all night. It made the night much easier to have somewhere to rest my back, and I slept."

As soon as her husband helped her to sit on the animal, I heard the sound of wings and the little swallow was back. It flew and chirped the way birds do in the early morning—a happy sound—and all of us found it a little easier to start walking. " 'O, that I had wings like a dove!'" I heard Mariam singing. "'I would fly away and be at rest.' Isn't the bird lovely?" Her husband's serious face opened up. He added in a sing-song voice that told me he too was quoting: "'Even the sparrow finds a home, and the swallow a nest for herself, where she may lay her young. . . .'"

Why did their words fill me with such longing? These young people, about to become parents, knew something the rest of us did not know, could not even guess. What was it? I remembered the preparations in the palace when a baby was expected and I shuddered. There was gold, and there were fine linens, and little beds and bowers of feathery softness, but there was no joy. So many of those babies had died as children and others in their youth. And there were whispers that all the young in Augustus's Roman household had been poisoned or drowned or killed in one way or another. Instead of joy, the coming of a baby brought fear and increased suspicion in the palace. The fear always centered on the throne: who would inherit it?

The years had given me the right to ask questions, so I did not hesitate. I asked Mariam: "You look so happy, my daughter. There is a radiance about you that I don't usually associate with expectant mothers. What is it that you know about your child? Is he due to inherit great wealth?"

Her face was serious. "Wealth?" she repeated as if examining the word. "The wealth of God's mercy, yes." She placed her hand on the waiting baby. "This is the Promised One," she added simply, expecting me to understand. "God's gift to us all."

I did not understand, yet nothing about her made me doubt her. So I decided to hide this bit of news and wait. Mariam and her husband were waiting for someone wonderful, with hope, with love, with utter trust. I wanted to catch some of that anticipation and keep it.

The swallow made a wide circle above our heads. She flew with what I would call joy. I was now convinced that she too was waiting for a wonder.

The Shepherd Father
Abiding in the fields

... and a little child shall lead them. (Isaiah 11:6b)

The LORD is my shepherd. ... (Psalm 23:1)

All we like sheep have gone astray. ... (Isaiah 53:6)

There's not much level land near Bethlehem and Jerusalem. We grow more rocks than barley on this soil. But the sheep like it; no matter how rough it is, they can find enough to eat, and sheep can graze anywhere.

Keeping sheep is not easy, but you get used to it after a while and the smell of them never leaves your clothes. You end up considering these creatures part of your family. I had started helping my father when I was a youngster, and I expected my own son to continue the family tradition. Not much to hope for, but it put food on the table most of the time. We shepherds are not despised but we come close to being ignored and everyone who can do something else will rush to that work instead of ours. It's very lonely having only sheep for company.

So I was glad when my son grew old enough to leave his mother and come with me to look after the sheep. He is a fine lad, a strong, quiet boy who, unlike me, spends much time thinking. His greatest ambition is to learn to read so he can study the great prophets. When he was little, someone in Bethlehem took an interest in him and spent time reading him the psalms and the prophets and the boy has not been the same ever since. I soon put a stop to that nonsense. What good is it to fill the boy's head with thoughts and hopes that are above him? Why make him miserable? I love the child and don't want him to forget where he comes from and where he will remain because of our poverty.

But on the lonely days when it rains on the hills and we huddle under our capes, or on those pleasant nights when we stay and sleep outside in the fields, the boy opens up and tells me stories. "Father, do you know that our prophets talk a lot about shepherds and their sheep?"

That interests me. "You mean there are people who can read and who talk about *us*?"

"Yes, that is exactly what I mean. They talk about our God being a shepherd and us being the sheep."

I look at him. "Is that so, son?"

"Yes, father. It is so," and his voice takes on a sound that makes me sad for him. I wish I could give him the hope of learning. His mind is so quick. I say, "But that is good. It does make me proud to think they call God our shepherd." My son, Jonathan, remains thoughtful. He says after a while, "But they also say that we—all of us—are like sheep who have gone astray."

I need to think about this. But I'm proud of my boy for telling me. In the night I hear him reciting, "The LORD is my shepherd; I shall not want. He maketh me to lie down in green pastures: he leadeth me beside the still waters. He restoreth my soul. . . ." I pretend I'm asleep because I hear the words and they comfort me. Another night, after a difficult day with the sheep, I hear him say, "All we like sheep have gone astray; we have all turned to our own way, and the LORD has laid on him the iniquity of us all." I keep myself very still to listen. Something hurts inside me.

Every night now I long to hear Jonathan speak the words of the prophets. So on that particular night, it seemed that all his words were coming together and what my son had dreamed was becoming reality.

We both saw the angel. We both heard the words. We came together in fear, trembling before God—that kind of fear—and tried to understand. "Did you hear it?" he wanted to know. "Do you also see what I see?" We had seen and we had heard.

"It's all those prophets you have been talking about, son—do you know that?" I asked him. I knew suddenly that he was right, that we had gone astray but now we were found. The angel's voice could not be denied. "Peace on earth," the angel kept singing, "good will toward human beings."

Jonathan looked at me in wild hope. For once I had put things together in my mind before he did. We ran to find God's hope together. My son had prepared me for the wonder of God's appearing.

So this is why when a learned man passed through Bethlehem asking for an apprentice I gave my blessings to Jonathan my beloved son to go learn from him. I thank God for him.

Jonathan
The shepherd boy and the night sky

In that region there were shepherds living in the fields, keeping watch over their flock by night. Then an angel of the Lord stood before them, and the glory of the Lord shone around them, and they were terrified. (Luke 2:8–9)

(My mentor, the man who rescued me from ignorance and educated me, has asked me to tell this story again and again. Now, finally, he is writing it down. I think he believes me. Will anyone else believe?)

"Father, Father, look!" I opened my mouth to cry it out as loud as I could but my voice refused to leave my mouth. I couldn't make a sound. The sky was filling with shapes of light never seen before. There was a constant movement above us, like a dance of the stars. Everything was lit up, yet the light was moving across the sky, like thousands of stars falling and rising, falling and rising. We were dumbfounded.

"This is the end of the world," I said, again without making a sound, "or the beginning of a new world." The sheep had fallen silent—that's the peculiar thing I remember. Usually, when a storm is coming, the sheep start a restless movement, not knowing where to turn, calling to each other, *Bah, Bah.* Instead of following a leader they turn here and there, here and there, making a racket. But on this night, they all stood still and looked to the skies. I wanted to laugh. Sheep looking to the sky? I hadn't seen that before. I was on the highest point of the pasture, and for a moment I looked down at the sheep, at my father, and all the other shepherds in distant meadows and hills. They were all looking to the sky.

And it was then that the music took shape and sounded like a song. Did I hear Hallelujahs? Did I hear Hosannas? Who knows? I will never be sure. But the sound was praise. This is what I can say for sure. Praise. The word "glory" took form and became something palpable. Not sadness, not laments, but joy and laughter, *Praise to God in the highest, glory, glory, glory.*

We fell on our knees. All of us. The sheep were still without voice, looking up at those moving lights. And we wept and trembled: was there ever a vision like this? Was there ever anything to prepare us for such glory? And despite the beauty and the glory, I suddenly knew that I was afraid. Filled with awe unspeakable. "The end has come," I said to myself, and then I wondered, "or is it a beginning?"

Later, when I found my voice, my father and I talked about what we had heard and we agreed on this: Through the songs and through the music and the motions of the stars we heard a voice. It sounded like my shepherd's flute, sweet and ethereal, but also deep, like an echo across valleys and hills, deep and resonant, something that came from a flute but echoed through an endless flute. It was a sound I will never hear again but one I will not forget even if I live an eternity.

The voice said, "Be not afraid." We agreed on this, Father and I. But what were the words? Did we hear words? We couldn't decide. We only knew that we had been told not to be afraid. And immediately our trembling ceased. I finally found the courage to run to my father and he enfolded me in his cape. "Father," I cried, but he said, "I know, son, I know." He was weeping. "Listen," he said, "the voice is speaking again."

"They are directing us somewhere," I said, and now I was laughing uncontrollably. "Father, let's go. I know where they are sending us."

Father grabbed a lamb and I picked up another. We started running and other shepherds joined us. We were all holding lambs, as if we were planning to offer gifts to someone, and we all were running.

We came to a cave I knew well. My friends and I had found shelter there many a time. The village of Bethlehem was tiny but there were huts and all kinds of little caves that gaped in the dry hills. I don't know why I was sure of the place, but I seemed to be directed there, and the lights of that night seemed to be brighter near this, my favorite cave.

A surprise was awaiting us. We entered carefully, the way people do when they step on holy ground. Father whispered, "You go on first, son, since you know the way." I tiptoed in, cradling my little lamb, which at that moment gave out a joyful *bah!* as if it had seen its mother, and danced in my arms. I put the lamb down and it pranced on uncertain legs to the interior. I followed. The unmistakable sounds of an infant startled me, and I stopped. But then I heard a man's voice say, "Whoever you are, know that you are welcome."

I motioned to the others to follow me, and we came to an opening where a young woman was sitting, holding a tiny baby, and a man, his face exhausted but joyous, was rushing toward us in welcome. We couldn't speak. Finally Father said, "A son, a savior, a promise," and he fell on his knees, sobbing now. The mother simply smiled at us and, still cradling the baby, made a movement with her arms as if offering him to us to see.

All the other shepherds fell on their knees, but my lamb was already there, licking the infant's tiny hands. I said to the mother, "Have you selected a name?"

"Yeshua," she whispered, "Savior."

"Do you know what is happening outside?" I asked her. "The heavens have opened."

"How?" she asked, and Joseph ran to the mouth of the cave and then he came back to her and he was weeping openly. "Mariam," he told her, "the angels of the Lord. . . ." But he couldn't finish.

"Yes," I said, "*they* told us to come here."

And then I heard the echo that had filled the sky and was entering this place, infusing and surrounding us: *Glory to God, and on earth, peace!* We all knelt and repeated the words. The baby looked at us as if he understood.

The Lamb
Jonathan's lamb meets
the Lamb of God

*Worthy is the Lamb that was slain to receive power, and riches,
and wisdom, and strength, and honour, and glory, and blessing.* (Revelation 5:12, KJV)

*Blessing, and honour, and glory, and power, be unto him that
sitteth upon the throne, and unto the Lamb for ever and ever.*
(Revelation 5:13b, KJV)

*This is a story told by a sage whom legend has called Balthazar; he,
together with other sages, visited Jesus soon after his birth.*

My children, listen with the ears of the heart and the imagi-
nation. Listen in order to understand. You sit around me, your eyes
shining, your lips parted ready to be fed, waiting for a story.
Tonight, instead of my voice, I want you to hear the voice of a
lamb. I met this lamb on a night when once long ago I saw a baby
like any other baby, but after I recognized him I knew he was like
no other baby. I want you to hear this story as the lamb would tell
it to you—if you could only hear his voice.

From the moment I slipped out of my mother's womb and
tried to stand on my spindly, crooked, shaky legs, I knew I
would die. It is bred in us, this knowledge of death.

We were out in the fields under the stars, and I felt my mother's tongue licking me, making me clean. Her breath was warm and her nose urged me on and on, ordering me to stand, to stand, to live. Why live if I am doomed to die? But she wanted me to live, so I found her source of milk and I forced it down, nudging it with my head, and then I opened my mouth and drank and drank. Why? In order to be slaughtered and to die?

I am a lamb. I like my name but not my fate.

The night of my birth was different from all others, my mother told me later. At night, animals like us are still. The dark falls and we sleep. The night fills with soft sounds— a cow coughs somewhere, a ewe moves, a horse snores. We lambs fold our legs under our bellies and we sleep.

But that night, sleep didn't come to any of us. The fields were alive with lights that moved and sang. My mother says that we all looked up, except for me, of course. I was too busy nursing. Even those other animals who stand on two legs were looking up. The milk was good, warm, and plentiful. I nursed well, and when I felt my belly full I stopped and moved from beneath my mother's shelter to sniff the world around me. All the animals stood on their four legs with head upturned, but there was no noise. Only songs. Had my mother forgotten me already? I nudged her again and she licked me some more, keeping me close beside her.

Then there was a lot of movement. The two-legged ones were running and my mother stirred, and I smelled her fear. Two hands snatched me. I heard my mother's startled *Bah!* and she started running, but I was not on my own legs. Someone else was holding me and running with me. I could hear the sound his legs made and I knew without being told that this was not an animal I recognized. I learned later that he was called a boy, a Shepherd Boy.

I heard my mother's cries, but the boy didn't seem to understand her. "He is too young for slaughter," she was crying. "Don't take him, don't take him. I promise to give you myself for meat after I have weaned him."

I felt sad for my mother. But, to tell you the whole truth, I was very excited. I was flying and being held. After a long while, we came to a stop. There were many of the two-legged ones among us, and they were holding other lambs whose mothers were running with mine, crying and begging for their little ones not to be slaughtered.

We stopped in front of a cave that smelled of animals. The Shepherd Boy was trembling now. I felt his heart beating next to mine. It sounded like a good heart, so I licked his hand. A man he called Father was talking to him, and the boy put me on the ground. But when we came to the entrance lit by that bright light from the skies that had followed us, I forgot all about him. My new legs felt strong and I danced my way inside. Something, some-one was calling me. I was followed in by a sound that sang, "The Lamb of God, the Lamb of God!" I liked hearing my name. But who was the Lamb of God? I knew they were not singing about me.

I thought I was alone, but soon I found out that many animals had followed me inside. I was the first one to reach him. It was a human baby held in the arms of his own mother. She was looking at me and smiling. I went straight up to the baby and licked his sweet hand. He stirred in his mother's arms. And I knew without being told that this was the Lamb of God. And I knew that he too was born to be led to the slaughter, just as I had been.

His mother turned to a man there and said, "Joseph, let us keep this one for Jesus to love." The man nodded and looked at me and then turned his eyes to the little baby. He looked sad for a moment, but the baby slept.

Later, when the baby grew into a little boy and we could understand one another, I heard him say as he petted me: "The Lamb of God who carries away the sins of the world." His voice was dreamy, and he often repeated sayings like this one. I did not know what the words meant, but I sensed they had to do with the slaughter I knew was coming. I was ready to die for him.

The sage finishes the story:

You are very quiet, my little ones. When I saw this baby Jesus I had already traveled many miles from that first night of the Lamb's birth. I and my fellows had followed a star that led us to him. Jesus was a few months old by then and could move his arms and hands and smile. The lamb was with him still. There was a mystery and wonder in the baby's presence and I called him King when I saw him. But that is another story. I offered Jesus a gift of myrrh, and it was on that night, when I lay down to sleep, that I heard the lamb telling me his story.

The Donkey
Its burden and its story

The donkey saw the angel of the LORD standing in the road, with a drawn sword in his hand; so the donkey turned off the road, and went into the field; and Balaam struck the donkey, to turn it back onto the road. (Numbers 22:23)

Then the LORD opened the mouth of the donkey, and it said to Balaam. . . . (Numbers 22:28a)

A speechless donkey spoke with a human voice and restrained the prophet's madness. (2 Peter 2:16b)

I have carried the burdens of humanity on my back. I am not a large animal—I cannot compare to a horse or an ox—but I have carried loads larger than myself through all the ages.

I don't have a handsome face and I don't even have a pretty voice, so there is nothing to make me attractive to anyone. In fact, my voice embarrasses me so much that I sing as loud as I can so as not to hear its ugliness. My voice cries out my pain and my anger, yet I like to see how it startles people. And then I fall quiet once again and trudge under the burdens of humanity. It is my fate.

In the night, trying to rest from the burdens of the day, after licking the wounds from the cruel whip, we tell stories to one another, we the tired field animals. I tell them how my name has become legendary. If a man is stubborn, they call him a donkey. If a man is rude, they call him an ass. Then we laugh together in our silent way and nod off. For we know that no animal is as stubborn as man.

Other nights, when we are not so tired and the evening is long and full of lingering light, I tell them the ancient story of Balaam and his famous ass, a story that has been carried inside the bones of our line for generation upon generation. Men cannot see the messengers of God as clearly as we can. How many of us have been beaten over and over again for stopping in the middle of the road! They don't know that we see what they don't see.

This is what I tell them: A long, long time ago, there was a man named Balaam. He was from Babylon, so he was supposed to be a seer. A nearby king wanted him to curse a new race that was spreading across the desert, the people we now know as Israelites. But as Balaam was riding my ancestor toward the place of curse, this marvelous ancestor saw an angel of the Lord and stopped. Of course he stopped! The angel held a sword and stood in a way that said clearly, *Do not pass.* But the man Balaam was blind to the messenger of the Lord. And so Balaam beat his donkey. This happened three times. Three times my ancestor was stopped by the angel of the Lord; three times he was beaten mercilessly by Balaam. But my ancestor would not disobey God's messenger; none of us ever has. When we see an angel, we know what we see. We don't have the blinded hearts of men. We can see the higher spirits.

So after the stoppings and the beatings, the Lord who created us—blessed be God's Name—opened my ancestor's mouth and he spoke so Balaam finally could understand. My friends, do you know that men don't realize we can speak to one another? Imagine such stupidity! And they call *us* dumb! So my famous ancestor spoke to the man Balaam and asked, "Why are you beating me? What have I ever done to you? You have ridden me all your life, and I have never treated you badly." So the man finally opened his true eyes and saw the angel of the Lord.

This is an old, old story, and I love to tell it. All of us donkeys have laughed about it throughout the ages. Every time we stop in the middle of the road and we are beaten, we remember Balaam's ass and are comforted.

But last night, a new story unfolded, and from now on my heart will sing it and pass it on through my bones to all who come after me. A child was born, and we animals may be the only ones who can tell this story.

It started out as an ordinary day, an ordinary story. I had brought a woman on my back along a long, dusty, and hilly road, a woman heavy with child. I felt a strange tingle when her husband helped her to sit on my back, and I was well pleased to offer her a seat and some rest in her condition.

They were good people, both the young woman and her husband. He never beat me, and she tried to dismount the moment darkness fell and then he hurried to give me hay and water. She patted my head and thanked me for giving her my back to sit on. So I was well satisfied to be of service to such grateful people. But even with such good omens, I could not have predicted what came next.

That night, the whole creation thrilled under the blessings of the Creator—blessed be God's Name! Something was being brought forth that was old as creation and new as the dawn of each day. We were tingling. I sensed it in every animal. I felt it in every particle of my tired body and refused to close my eyes for sleep. A baby was born and everything changed for the better.

The woman I had carried gave birth. I, the humble and ridiculed donkey, had carried the woman who gave birth to One I recognized. One who has been with us from the beginning. A baby with such connection to the Creator of the world—blessed be God's Holy Name—that we animals recognized him instantly. We the humble, the despised, the beasts of burden recognized him.

So last night, instead of crying, I sang for the first time, and I liked my voice.

The Babylonian *Magos*
Reading the stars and planets

When I look at your heavens, the work of your fingers,
the moon and the stars that you have established;
what are human beings that you are mindful of them,
mortals that you care for them? (Psalm 8:3–4)

The one who made the Pleiades and Orion. . .
the LORD is his name. . . . (Amos 5:8)

"Where is the child who has been born king of the Jews? For
we observed his star at its rising, and have come to pay him
homage." (Matthew 2:2)

Night after night for months I have been following the travels
of great Zeus, the king planet of the skies. As darkness falls each
night, I watch him rise in the east to sail slowly, imperceptibly,
among the fixed stars. *Planétes,* the Wanderer, the Greeks called
him from their vantage point across the wide sea, and I, here
in the desert, must agree with the name. Yet I know something
they, with their cool logic, cannot guess. The Greeks lack the
gift of mystery that unlocks the secrets of the East. Do they
sense the immense restlessness in the heavens these days and
nights? The planets reveal it to us who spend the night hours
studying them. Zeus—let me call him Jupiter for the sake of the

Romans who control our world—is moving toward his father Kronos; the Romans know him as Saturn. The moon sails close to them, and as together they enter the Aries constellation, and the constellation nears the sun, I tremble, for they are all portents of the coming of a great king. My heart begins to flutter as I study the heavens, and I get myself ready for a journey. I set out with my servant and two loaded camels. The lords of the heavens are speaking: a king is born or is about to be born.

Why am I saying this? There is an old, old prophecy among the Jews—and I have met many of that race both in my native Babylon and in my wanderings—that out of Judah another great king will be born. I must go to find out the truth of this prophecy, of this coming. I have been in Egypt for a few months trying to learn what they know about Helios, the Sun, and it is now time to depart. As I set out through the desert, east of Heliopolis, on the endless and dangerous Sinai, I find rest in the oasis of Themed, well known to desert travelers. A humble inn there has welcomed people like me—I am known as a *magos* in the land of my birth—for generations. That first night several of us stayed under the stars for long hours after nightfall. This is why we prefer the desert. There is nothing to obstruct our view of the stars, and nowhere else do they shine with such brightness.

The inn is filled with wise men of profound learning. The life of the *magos* is of necessity lonely. Whenever I have reached this place, I have enjoyed the company of others in my chosen profession of stargazing, of measuring the skies, of telling the future, and of thinking. The Greeks call us students of the stars, astrologers.

Tonight there are quite a few of us astrologers gathered in this rare oasis. I hear murmurs, I hear some questions, some softly spoken discussions. But after darkness falls most of the travelers retire to the shelter of the inn as the night chill falls on the desert. I remain under the stars.

Three other travelers linger outside. Like me, they must be loath to leave such a brilliant sky to lie under a roof. We find ourselves coming together, comparing notes.

"I have also come from Heliopolis," a man with darker skin than the rest of us says, "but my origin is farther south, in Ethiopia."

"And I come from Persia," a venerable *magos* bows his head toward us.

"I have been traveling across the sea and land, all the way from Crete," a man with strong Greek features announces. We let our servants take care of the animals and we make ourselves comfortable under the stars to confer through the night.

Three of us have heard of the prophecies, for long memories of Abram's race linger in these parts. The Greek is more skeptical, but the movement of Zeus has entranced him. We interpret the Babylonian zodiac to him and then, with the usual avid curiosity of the Greeks, he asks for details. When he hears of the prophecy concerning the Jews, he says in the decisive manner of his people: "We must leave immediately for the heart of Judah. If the stars tell us of the coming of a king, we must be there to welcome him."

"I would like to offer homage," the Persian says, but still hesitates. We of the East do not make decisions in haste.

"I am compelled to bow down and worship him," says the gentle Ethiopian, "because the movements of the heavenly objects give me an urgency I have not felt before, but we must study them further. . . ."

And so, through the night, we remain outdoors discussing our findings from the perspective of our diverse origins. The Greek is ready to move, but the rest of us are hesitant. And then, before full light arrives, the morning star rises in the East and our decision is made for us. "It is Jupiter," I whisper in awe, "the morning star."

"It is not a star," the Greek says in the pedantic manner of his race. "It is *Planétes,* the Great Wanderer; Zeus is on the move."

There is awe in the voice of the Persian when he announces, "My brothers, the time has come, for the morning star, Zeus the *Planétes*"—he bows to the Greek—"is in the constellation of Aries." Now his voice trembles.

The Ethiopian stands up and then bends his body deeply before the slow-rising star. "A king is born," he says. "All the portents agree. The time has come."

We awaken our servants and by the first light we have set our faces toward Jerusalem, for that is where King Herod resides. Is the new king a member of his family? We must find out. We follow the King's Highway.

The days are long and harsh through the desert, but the blue waters of Eilat refresh us after the merciless kilometers in the Sinai. Then we start the long upland trek toward the plateaus and the spectacular gorges of the northern route. It is springtime and we do not suffer much from the heat, but we must be in constant watch for possible sudden rainfalls that cause floods and disaster in the deep, dry river beds. We have increased our numbers with donkeys that know how to follow routes in leading the less intelligent camels. All four of us have hired guides who know how to read the desert and the gorges as we know how to read the ancient scrolls. It is important that we arrive safely. Our camels are loaded with gifts for the new king.

The kilometers are not long but the way is rough; our Persian friend is old in years and we take care not to weary him. It takes us a month to arrive in Philadelphia, north and east of the great East Sea of the desert, the one the locals call Salt. From there we move to Jericho and then hurry to Jerusalem. Our visit with King Herod fills us with a strange unease. His own sages, who are forbidden from reading the stars but who have read their own scribes, announce to him, with great trepidation, that the king the Hebrew prophets wrote about is to be born in Bethlehem. They do not call him king but Messiah. The Greek explains to us that they mean *Christós*, the Anointed One. Herod seems highly interested and asks us to return to him with the news of the child. So we continue on our way but stop briefly outside the city to rest before walking the ten kilometers that lead to Bethlehem.

When we wake it is still dark. We look to the south and see the great planet once again, brighter this time than when we bowed to him in the desert. Kronos has joined Zeus, and fiery Ares, the Roman Mars, adds his light to theirs. We move toward this light, overjoyed to see it again. We know we have come to the right place when it hovers and, to our eyes, seems to stop above a humble house. Trembling, we enter. "Hail, King of the Jews!" we cry as we kneel before a child who is smiling at us from the arms of his serene mother. We weep for joy and offer our gifts.

King Herod
His troubled dreams

In the time of King Herod, after Jesus was born in Bethlehem of Judea.... (Matthew 2:1a)

In the days of King Herod of Judea.... (Luke 1:5)

Ugh, I am so sick of my family. Terrible shedding of blood covers and pollutes us all. What vultures I have produced, what imbeciles for sons.

You think these are the ravings of an old man, don't you? Well, you may be right. But I am still the king and only I have the power of life and death over them all. Antipater is due to die tomorrow. What irony in the name. Anti-pater—against his father. We have used the name in this cursed family enough. It should have been an omen.

It has taken me years and years to establish a kingdom of power and honor in Judea. Yes, you heard me right—honor! Look how the Romans favor me. This is what I wanted for Judea, something to rival Rome. I have come close. Have you seen the Temple, my Temple? Greater than any building outside Athens and Rome, beautiful enough to rival the Parthenon. And still the Jews call me an Idumean, a son of Esau, not a son of Jacob, and argue with me about every detail, even the Roman eagle over the Temple's gates. Sometimes the fickle people love me; then they turn around, and they hate me. All that matters to *me* is that they fear me. My sons wait for my death, and all that I have created may collapse around them when

I am gone. They don't understand the delicate craft of ruling. The craft of ruling, ah! How I have loved it, and it hasn't betrayed me.

I'm a bitter and a sick old man now—despite all the wealth, despite all the palaces, I'm a bitter old man now. My only regret? The death of my beautiful, my beloved Mariamne. How I loved that girl. But even *she* betrayed me and I was right to have her killed, and her two sons. . . *our* two sons. Bah, what does it all mean? What does it mean to love one's offspring? I do not know. There is no love in this family; there never has been any love in this family. They all deserved to die.

But every now and then, in the middle of the night, I remember Mariamne and the children and remember how much I loved them once. Just for a moment, I long to know the meaning of the word again—but then the moment passes and I remember all those who are plotting against me. The only thing that matters is this: holding on to the throne. There hadn't been a king of Judea for so long. But I, I was named king by Augustus himself. *The king of Judea.* Be careful, they tell me, don't call yourself "the Jewish king; these crazies will never accept you."

So this is what I am—the great king of Judea. I have brought them peace and I have brought them wealth, so it is not right that I should die. My body is rotting, but I am not ready to die. Maybe I will not. Someone as great as I should not have to die. Look at how many I have killed to keep the throne. So much blood, so much killing. Was it all for nothing?

The dreams trouble me. The one last night—was it a dream, or did it really happen as I dreamt it? I dare not find the answer. My soothsayers are hovering, and I am thinking of having them killed for being such fools, for not knowing about the birth ahead of time. I see them now—the sycophants. They are fawning and thinking up excuses for not understanding the prophecies, so maybe I didn't dream it, maybe those wise foreigners, those impostors, did indeed visit me last night.

I have received countless potentates but never any that reminded me of kings and philosophers bound in one. I have known the

Nabateans; I have walked the stones of Petra. At first I thought that was where they came from, that Aretas had sent them. But they made no claims and said not a word about their origin—only that they were from the East.

Their dress was modest, but their horses, I was told, were laden with gold and perfumes. When I received the word, I knew the gifts were for me. But then the visitors came into my presence and their words were like a blow to the chest. I have not recovered my breath yet.

"Where is the child?" they asked. "We long to bow down and worship him."

"The child? What child?" *What have my sons done now?* I wondered. Was a grandson born? Did they plot to take my throne, to give it to him?

"No, no," the weird ones answered. "This child will rule but will not kill. This child will have a power given to no king before him, but he will have within him the weakness that leads to early death. Yet his kingdom will have no end. This child gives life but chooses death for himself. A king who serves as a slave," they said. *Gibberish,* I thought, *the nonsense of foreign dreamers.* At least my own fools can read the books, and they may be more reliable than the stars.

"It was the star that told us of his coming," the foreign *magoi* explained only to baffle me. "It told us of a Jewish king." At that I froze. I bellowed for my own soothsayers. They offered no help but shook from head to toe, avoiding my eyes. "Something about Bethlehem," they stammered when I pressed them, "the town is in the holy books—about a child to be born there, a Messiah who will govern with justice and peace. . . ."

"That's me," I yelled at them. "*I* have brought you peace." So I sent the Eastern fools on to Bethlehem to see for themselves. And here I sit waiting for them to return. If there *is* a child he will not live long. No one but me has the power of the king. But oh, if I could only live forever. Suppose this child has the power to let me live forever? Or is this only my dream? What do you say, you fools? What do the stars say?

The Greek *Magos*
Escaping Herod's clutches

And having been warned in a dream not to return to Herod,
they left for their own country by another road. Now after they
had left, an angel of the Lord appeared to Joseph in a dream
and said, "Get up, take the child and his mother, and flee to
Egypt." (Matthew 2:12–13)

We had called the little boy "King of the Jews," and his parents looked surprised. After we worshiped him, we opened our treasure boxes and offered him gifts that made his mother laugh. It did seem strange if you looked at it dispassionately: a young girl with only beauty and purity as ornaments, a father with callused hands, a humble home, probably on rent, and an ordinary baby boy. Yet we had called him "King of the Jews," despite all appearances. "King?" the father inquired. "Let us hope Herod and his court don't hear you use this title!"

"But we have already seen King Herod," I explained, "and he is eager to know about the child, so that he may also offer him homage." The man turned to look at the mother, and I saw fear in her eyes, but the baby gurgled and she was at peace again.

We took our leave reluctantly and found our camel drivers and servants in the outskirts of Bethlehem. They had set up one of the tents, offered us dinner, and then we entered together in the one tent to save time, so we could rest before returning to Jerusalem.

My eyelids grew heavy and I noticed that the Persian *magos* was already asleep, his head resting on his chest. The others were making themselves comfortable on pallets. I decided to allow myself to sleep, though I felt agitation and excitement after the day's events.

But with only an hour's rest, I woke up with a start, feeling deeply troubled. I sat up and looked around me. My three companions, who by this time had become my friends, were also waking though I had made no noise. In the light of the oil lamp, we looked at one another.

"Friends," the Persian *magos*, the oldest among us, said in a voice that was shaky, "I had a most uncomfortable dream."

"I also," said the energetic Babylonian, who looked wide-eyed and surprised.

"I must confess that I have awakened from a most troubling dream," murmured the gentle Ethiopian. They all turned to look at me.

"We don't read the stars as well as you do," I confessed, "but we pay close attention to dreams. And this dream is not one to be ignored. I have been ordered not to return to Jerusalem, but by whom, I cannot tell."

"It is the angel of the Lord of the Heavens," said the Ethiopian. "I saw his fiery sword, or maybe it was the brilliance of his arm, barring the way."

The Babylonian was very quiet—rather unusual for him. Finally he spoke, sadly: "The angel of the Lord barring the way. . . . It reminds me of an old, old story, dear friend from distant Ethiopia. I too received a very strong message that it is King Herod who is seeking to kill the holy child we have seen and worshiped." The kind man looked deeply shaken.

We all deferred to the eldest and wisest among us, the Persian *magos*. "It must have been the angel Michael," he continued quietly, "blessed be his name. Our friend from Crete is correct. We have been warned and we have been forbidden from returning through Jerusalem. King Herod has not hesitated to kill his own children when he thought his throne was threatened. His desire to find this child must mean that he wants to destroy him. We must warn the parents and we must depart by leaving for Gaza immediately. It is not a dark night. Herod will not suspect that we have left for the coast."

I offered to warn the parents. I was the youngest among them and my curiosity about the young family had not yet been satisfied. Why did this child-king arrive in such humble circumstances? What was behind the secrecy? And why did the lords of Heaven, both stars and angels, involve themselves in announcing his coming and in warning us of danger?

I took only one servant with me. The village was not large, so it didn't take me long to find the small house again. The sky was bright. I knocked on the door and the man opened it a crack, lifted a lamp and looked at me with caution. He recognized me and opened the door for me but closed it immediately behind me. The room was in disarray. We were whispering so as not to waken mother and child who were sleeping behind a partition. "Are you making preparations for departure?" I asked. He nodded. "I have been warned in a dream," he said. "I must take the child and his mother and leave for Egypt." I was too stunned to speak for a while.

"Joseph," I said after recovering my speech. "Who warned you? I was coming here to do that myself. We have all been troubled by dreams about Herod's intentions toward the child."

"Yes," he said, "this child. . . ." He choked for a few minutes and could not continue. He was bundling some possessions while he tried to explain. "From the very beginning nothing has been ordinary. We are becoming accustomed to the messages of angels regarding him." He smiled and shook his head. "His advent was announced to my wife and then to me; his birth was surrounded by apparitions, songs, and movements in the heavens. And now, when I was thinking that both mother and child are ready for the return to Nazareth, you and your companions appear to fill us with foreboding. How can you possibly know of the birth of the King of the Jews when Herod is still on his throne?" He looked at me as if lost for a moment, his eyes with a faraway look, but what I saw there was not fear but awe.

I said, "We are students of the stars," but he did not let me finish.

"We are not allowed to study the stars," he said.

"I know, Joseph, but hear me out. This was not an ordinary portent. We spent hours—no, weeks—discussing what we had learned, searching your writings and ours, discovering astounding prophecies. I was rather skeptical but very impressed by the knowledge of my friends, the *magoi*. After seeing you and the child and the mother yesterday, however, it was not knowledge that mattered to me, but this awareness of the unknown—of wonder. I was convinced as I looked at the child that he will not be a king like any other. We said this much to Herod, but I think he scoffed. The power of this child when he grows will not be of the sword or of armies; his strength will come from what the world deems weakness—from agapé, love."

"Yes," he agreed, "it is both my hope and my fear. But now we must think of saving his life. Herod will soon suspect you are not going back to him. His men may already be on the way."

Then I knew why I had come. I said, "Joseph, my friends are indeed from the East and they will return there. But I must go back to Egypt and from there to my home across the sea. The gorges and the deserts from here to Egypt are extremely difficult to traverse and dangerous for a young mother with a child. You cannot do it alone. I offer you the protection of my caravan. Will you come with me?"

Relief washed over Joseph. "God indeed has sent you, friend," he said, and he went to prepare mother and child for the long journey. And I was filled with gratitude and wonder.

The Innkeeper's Granddaughter
A story from Bethlehem

*And she gave birth to her firstborn son and wrapped him in
bands of cloth, and laid him in a manger, because there was no
place for them in the inn.* (Luke 2:7)

Yes, yes, this is the place. Come in out of the cold and rest a bit,
will you? Nowadays, visitors come and ask to be shown it, so I've
got used to the question. It's still strange to me, but if folks want
to look at a stable, why should I say no? Both Mama and
Grandma taught me to give a cup of water to a stranger. You are
welcome. See, I've built a fire in the middle of the stable and cook
and take my meals in here these days, since so many of you come
asking to be shown the place.

How did it happen? Well, I'll tell you. I've heard the story
often enough, you see. When times were hard and there was no
one traveling hereabouts after the sack of Jerusalem—some ten
years ago it must have been—and we were hungry and cold in
the winters, Grandma would have us gather 'round her, hand us the
last piece of dry bread to munch on, and then she'd tell us the story.
We never tired of it. She told it so as to make us forget the hunger,
but we loved to hear it anyway. You know how children never tire
to hear the same story over and over again?

The wonder is how any of you have heard of it! There was a feller a few years back, before the sack it was, come through here carrying his writing things and he happened upon us one day, asking many questions. Had we heard of a baby born around these parts, some eighty years or so back it was, he said, and Mama laughed and told him Grandma's story. He must have put it down in writing somewhere, and you folks must have heard of it, eh?

I thought as much. Well, let me tell it the way I heard it as a child, 'cause that's the best way. The eyes and ears of a child are like none other.

"Children," she'd start, "'tis not the inn that brought us good fortune, 'tis the stable."

And Mama, knowing her cue, would say, "But look at it now, Ma, there's nothing in it now. Where's the good fortune?"

"Well, times are hard. We had to sell the donkey and eat the rest of the animals. One or two of them were there when the baby was born, so they lived a long while. Sometimes I thought they too remembered, especially the donkey. I heard it died the moment we sold it, died when it was forced to leave this stable. I always thought the donkey remembered that baby."

"The baby? What baby, Grandma?" We would cry it out, knowing our cue.

"The baby whose mother blessed me, that's who. Let me recount the story. Those days were better than these. The Romans left us pretty much alone to do as we pleased as long as those hotheads, the Zealots, didn't cause trouble. Augustus was still the great king and he was good to us. That old Herod, the famous one, he brought us some peace too, so the inn did good business. Bethlehem may be small, but lots of folks traveled through here to get to Jerusalem. And that year, we had more custom than ever before, 'cause the great king called for a census. We had been born here, so we stayed. But many a family returned from other parts to register, since this was their birthplace.

"I remember that one day. I was so tired from all the running around and all the cooking, I was ready to drop, but I had to slaughter a couple more lambs before I could stop, so they'd be ready for the morrow. We had lots of people to feed. Your Grandpa went to the door one more time, to close it, I think, and I heard his voice say, 'Sorry, young man, there's no room left here. They are all taken—every space for sleeping is full. I've nowhere to put you.' And the stranger's voice quiet but strong came through to where I was standing—'My wife is with child; I think her time has come.'

"I moved to the door to take a look. The girl looked ready to fall off her feet. And the baby had already dropped. I knew it. What could I do? I felt so sorry for her. I said to your Grandpa, 'I'm going to the stable to bring some more straw for the beds tomorrow,' and motioned to the tired couple to follow me. I said to the man, 'I know the stable isn't as good as the inn, but it's quiet here, and we can make your wife comfortable with lots of good clean straw.'

"He was so grateful, it touched me, so I said to him, 'When her time comes, and it'll be soon, throw this stone against the door, and I'll come a-running to give you a hand.'

"He said, 'I'll need some help cutting the cord. If you could come then. . . .' I said I'd do better than that and rushed back to the inn before your Grandpa missed me." Grandma always stopped there, thoughtful-like, and we cried out as we always did, "Go on, Grandma, tell us what happened next. Did the baby come?"

She had a dreamy look then. "Ah, yes, the baby came. . . but I didn't need the father to call me to come help. Something else did it."

"What was it, Grandma, what was it?"

And always here she would pause again and look at each one of us and the awe would be in her voice as she whispered, "It was the angels of the Lord, my children, the angels of the Lord." And we would hush and try to imagine.

It seems to me Grandma must have been struck by some kind of light that night. Grandpa never said he saw the angels, and none of the people staying at the inn made any claim to have seen them. So Mama always said, "Only your Grandma heard the songs and saw the sky filled with light." Why was it so? "My mother's heart was good," Mama would answer, "so God gave her the favor and let her hear the song."

What *was* the song? Well, that's the real mystery, isn't it? It was all about the baby born that night in a manger. Grandma did go to cut the cord and to give them something to drink and eat. And while she was here, inside the stable, all of it happened—the lights and the songs, and the animals bleating and mooing and dancing! When we asked what were the angels like, she could never tell us. Her eyes would fill with tears, a faraway look in them, and her voice would whisper a song: "Good news, good news, peace on this earth, peace. . . ." And then she'd weep, and we'd leave her alone for a while.

One time only I heard her asking herself, "I wonder what happened to them—the young girl and her child, and that good man who took care of them? With all the joy that night, their lives must have been good."

So why are you folks interested? Why do *you* want to see the stable where he was born? Do *you* have the answer?

Symeon
He waits for the promise and is not disappointed

Lord, you now have set your servant free
to go in peace as you have promised;
For these eyes of mine have seen the Savior,
whom you have prepared for all the world to see. . . .
(The Book of Common Prayer, 120)

It had been revealed to him by the Holy Spirit that he would not
see death before he had seen the Lord's Messiah. (Luke 2:26)

The years are passing like a fleeting thought, one of our psalmists sang. How well he understood the passage of time. What I only guessed in my youth, I know from experience in my old age. I wake up every morning, and before I have time to finish praying, the day is gone!

I have lived a long time. I have walked humbly before my God, but I am not ready to depart. Let me explain why.

Years back, when my youth was already past, and I was content to spend hours praying in the Temple, the Holy Spirit came upon me and filled me with a conviction that nothing since has dispelled, not even the passage of time. I recognized the voice I heard, though I had never heard it before. It was as welcome as life-giving water when the throat is parched, as reliable as the sun who is the harbinger of day. I knew that the voice I heard was that of God's messenger. It said, "Thus says the Lord: Symeon, my servant, you have lived a righteous life and your devotion to me rises like the prayers of a clean heart. I promise that you will not know death before you have seen the Lord's anointed." I fell on my knees and stayed there for the rest of that night.

The next morning I woke up filled with joy, and much of it still remains within me despite the many years that have visited me since then—the joy of anticipation, the wonder of God's promise. Whenever parents bring a firstborn to the Temple, at the time of purification, I tremble and I ask: "Is this the one, O Lord?" But the answer is never yes, not even maybe. It is as if a voice says, "When you see him here, there will be no need for questions."

Today I woke up trembling, scarcely able to walk. My eyesight is weakening; everything now blurs before me. I long for our God's anointed, but will I be able to see him when the time comes? Is this the day for me to die? I then remember the promise and know once again that my time has not yet come. But it is fast approaching.

With the help of a grandson I climb the highest hill of Jerusalem and look south toward Bethlehem. I remain there until dark. I am waiting, waiting for the Lord.

And I am not disappointed. Even with my poor eyesight I see much movement in the heavens—lights and more lights, as if the stars are falling only to suspend over the city of David. Is this the time, Lord? I ask, and I know that the answer is *Yes.* My grandson and I spend the night on the hill drinking in the light. All the prophets speak of light, and I know that God's anointed will lead us to the Light. The time is very near. A few days, I tell my grandson, a few days before they bring him to the Temple. I must return there now to wait for the Lord's anointed. My arms will hold the holy child. My dim eyes will perceive him. And then I will be able to depart in peace, for my eyes will have seen God's salvation.

Anna the Prophet
Her last words

At that moment she came, and began to praise God and to speak about the child to all who were looking for the redemption of Jerusalem. (Luke 2:38)

When my husband died, I was still a girl. My family grieved for me, but I did not feel the grief or the abandonment of widowhood. I knew the Lord God had other dreams for me, other roads I should travel. My parents wanted to find me a second husband, but I refused. No, I said, no; not all of us are destined for marriage, and not all women need to have children. A few of us must remain single to serve the Lord without distraction.

They were astounded, they were angry and confused, and they spoke harsh words to me. But what is more important? To obey God or to conform to the ideas and customs of men? I had such an assurance in my heart that I belonged to God that nothing anyone said could frighten me into changing. I was free. I uttered a fond farewell to the memory of my husband, I thanked him for setting me free, and I departed for Jerusalem. I entered the Temple and offered to serve there, hidden from the eyes of the world but useful to all who came to worship. Much work needed to be done in the Women's Court, and I did it with gladness.

When they tell the story of the coming of the Child, they will tell you about the man who welcomed him at his presentation, about old Symeon, who held the baby in the Temple. I wonder if anyone will remember a very old woman who could barely walk but who prophesied?

A friend who could figure out these things told me that I was eighty-four years of age. I had stopped counting a long time before. I needed very little food, and fasting had become a blessed habit with me. It helped me pray with more attention. On this last year of my life, I spent most of the day praying—I could not wash or scrub floors any longer—and during my prayers I was filled with the assurance that the coming of God's anointed was very near. I had been asleep in the tiny room I had occupied for years at the Women's Court when I felt the strong urge to go into the main hall of the court. There I saw Symeon, a familiar presence, a man whose constant praying reminded me of myself, and I knew that the time had come. His face was bathed in tears and he was holding an infant in his arms. I knew that Symeon's vision was poor, so I was glad that he could hold the child so he could see him through the touch of his hands.

Symeon was praying aloud, thanking God, and immediately his words thrilled me: "Now let your servant depart in peace," he was crying, "for my eyes have seen your salvation, O God."

I approached and asked Symeon to hand the child to me so the old man could talk to the parents. The little one was strong, alert, looking around as though he understood what was happening. For the first and only time in my long life I felt a moment's sadness that I had never had a baby. But then, when I knew that I was holding God's promise, God's anointed, I was visited by such joy, such peace and reassurance, that the regrets disappeared. I took the baby around to all who were present, telling them that this was the redemption of Jerusalem, and all the while I could still hear Symeon. Filled with prophecy, he was telling the mother of the child that her son was a sign from God and that the thoughts of many would be revealed because of him. Then his voice changed; he turned to her and looked into her eyes, and for a moment I thought he could really see her—her own eyes wide open, her sweet sad and smiling face—as he said to her with great sorrow, "And a sword shall pierce your own soul also." I saw her turn to her husband with tears and questions, but he only shook his head, bewildered.

So I approached and placed the baby back into his mother's arms and took her aside. I said, "My girl, my daughter, this is the time for rejoicing; this is the time for praise. You are blessed indeed among women. Hold on to that. The time for sorrow is ahead for you, but it is so for all women, and for all men. But yours is the child of hope, and this is what you should hold on to. I pray for you as my last act on this earth—that you will enjoy this child and not grieve, that you will forget the prophecies so that you can be a mother, a mother! Keep all these things in your heart, my daughter, but do not grieve and do not be afraid. Now go home. Love and enjoy your child. He needs you."

My own time has come and I am at peace. I wait for my Lord. "Now let your servant depart in peace."

Luke
The evangelist's last story

His mother treasured all these things in her heart. (Luke 2:51b)

And the child's father and mother were amazed at what was being said about him. (Luke 2:33)

I had not planned to write this account, but after meeting the aged Mariam, mother of the beloved Jesus, I had no choice. Her story was so compelling that I started going around Palestine asking questions about her son and his short life. Writing my two books was inevitable after these encounters: meeting the people whose lives and spirits were transformed because of the Lord Jesus transformed my life also. Where is the beginning? Is it with Mariam, his chosen mother? How can I add to what I have already written?

She lived a long life, not something she had expected or even desired, as she told me, but she was content to complete the span that the Lord had intended for her. She was tiny by then, her skin wrinkled, her back bent, but every now and then as she spoke I could see the sparkle in the eye that brought to mind the young, spirited girl she was recalling.

She was deeply moved as she recounted her story and at times highly amused to hear from me the rumors that were already spreading about her throughout the communities of faith. She said with a fervor that must have echoed that of her youth, "There is nothing magical about the Lord's works, nothing that would ever remind us of the gods of the pagans. Yes, I did see angels. Yes, I did hear their song. But this was not magic—it was the work of the Spirit."

Throughout our long conversations, she was more drawn to the memory of the early years than the terror and suffering at the end of her son's life. It was left to others to tell me of the agonies in the garden and the miracle at the tomb. His mother was delighted to relive the wonder of her son's coming. It was she who helped me see the night when the skies opened and the angels of the Lord broke out into unrestrained songs of joy and promise.

But I wanted to lead her even further back, to the days when she was a young girl, waiting. It was not something she could describe willingly. She was hesitant and a bit shy about it, but after I asked her about the visitation of the angel, she walked to the window and looked outside for a long time. When she turned and spoke, her eyes were no longer seeing me. They were filled with a light I could not quite endure. She asked me, "Have you ever seen an angel, Brother Luke?" and I felt the shiver she must have felt at the encounter because of what I heard in her voice. I was to hear the word messenger, *angelos,* from others as I sought my story, but it was that first time the word filled me with awe. What must she have felt as a young girl being visited by an angel?

"It is the brightness," she said. "There is no way you can mistake that light for anything other than the light that emanates from the Creator. It must be the reflected radiance of God's brightness. Our ancestors have told us that man cannot see God and live, so what we see is the reflected brightness. And *that* we can survive. But the other part of the encounter that I find so difficult to talk about was the promise of peace. We knew it for a while, Joseph and I, during the years Jesus lived with us. It was when Jesus became convinced of his calling that I started trembling for him and lost my peace."

I wanted to interrupt, to ask about the words and the appearance of the angel, but how could I? She was lost in memories of sweetness mingled with awe. How could I enter there? Every now and then she would speak and I could tell she was quoting words she had never forgotten. "Be joyful, you who are filled with grace," she quoted, and then she laughed. "Two words in the Greek which I could suddenly understand. *Khaire keharitoméni.* Two words that changed me and all who came to know my son and who will come to know him. Can you imagine what it means to be told that you have found favor with God? From that moment on it was as if something opened in my heart and all these words and promises fell into that opening to be kept as a treasure that never tarnishes."

Mariam paused a moment, lost in thought, before she continued. "But it was a treasure that I usually forgot about. Before his coming, I did not forget it even for a minute. They were always with me, the angel's promises of peace and of salvation. But afterward I forgot them because I could not bear to remember, since so little had changed. And then, when he went on his mission, I did not speak of them because all of us—even his closest friends and I—didn't seem to recognize who he was at times. *We human beings want to see the miracle we expect, not the one God has in store for us.* Do you see the difference? My son Jesus was the only one who could enter into the mind of God, and it was this that others could not accept in him. It terrified them because it did not meet their expectations."

I sat there taking notes and listening to her, even though I felt a kind of trembling inside me also. Then she came close to me and said very quietly, "During the nine months of waiting I was sure of who he was. I was at peace, waiting for this wonder that God had chosen to reveal only to me. That waiting, that assurance, was what helped me endure all that was to come. Do you begin to understand?"

James
A brother tells his story

"Where did this man get this wisdom and these deeds of power? Is not this the carpenter's son? Is not his mother called Mary? And are not his brothers James and Joseph and Simon and Judas? And are not all his sisters with us? Where then did this man get all this?" And they took offense at him. (Matthew 13:54b–57a)

Then he appeared to James, then to all the apostles. (1 Corinthians 15:7)

. . . and when James and Cephas and John, who were acknowledged pillars, recognized the grace that had been given to me. . . . (Galatians 2:9a)

He was my brother and I loved and resented him. Even as a young boy, in our large extended family, I knew that he was better than the rest of us—more fair, more just, more disciplined, and certainly more obedient. But he was also kind and funny and made an effort not to take himself seriously, something at which I never succeeded. Yeshua—Jesus, as you know him—was my brother. To declare this seems difficult today because my name for him now is "the Lord." It is a far cry from the names I called him in my youth.

We were a large family and got along well in Nazareth. The whole town knew us because they respected our father Joseph, and our mother was everybody's friend and helper. When our father died, Jesus took over the support of the family. By then the girls were married and had moved out. We, the two eldest, stayed at home, not willing to leave our mother alone, working in the carpentry shop and making the necessary furniture for our sisters' new homes.

It was in those last years that I started resenting my brother Jesus. He spent too much time in prayer, in reading the prophets, and in visiting various rabbis around Galilee. He would return in deep thought, and at those times I couldn't get a word out of him. Frequently, he looked as if he were far away from all of us. The rumors about the activities of our cousin John didn't help matters any. Jesus became increasingly focused on whatever it was he was contemplating, and I left home for a while to get away from him and to find out if what we were hearing about our cousin John was true. The son of Elizabeth and Zechariah was preaching in the wilderness across the Jordan.

John's message drew me and I was tempted to stay with him, but I had other responsibilities. My plan was to go to Jerusalem to find work in the great city. My desire was to be near the Temple.

When I returned home to marry and say goodbye to the family, I shared with them what I had seen and heard from John. All that Nazirite discipline and severity appealed to me, but as soon as I repeated some of John's words at home, I knew that Jesus would be the one to go to the wilderness; he was ready to leave us. His face lit up at the news from the prophet, and he started preparing our mother for his departure. I offered to accompany him.

Our mother gave us permission to go in peace. We kissed her goodbye and started out on the road together. Jesus didn't say much, but his thinking was so intense that I could almost hear it. At one point I said to him, "You are not going back to Nazareth, are you?" He was startled and didn't speak for a while. Then he said, as if to himself, "Will Nazareth receive me?" I decided not to ask any more questions. I was curious to observe his reaction to John, who dressed in skins and ate wild honey for sustenance. But none of us could have anticipated what met us there in the wilderness.

There was a large crowd around John, who was in the process of baptizing a number of his followers. My brother was very quiet, riveted by the scene before him. He had a stillness about him which, when intensified, came to me in waves that made me more uncomfortable than ever in his presence. Whatever it was, John felt it also, for he suddenly emerged from the water and came toward us, crying out, "Here is the Lamb of God who takes away the sin of the world!" I was furious. I went up to him and whispered fiercely, "John, it's only my brother, Jesus. What are you doing? What are you saying?" But John, trembling from head to toe, was gazing only at Jesus. Jesus looked at him with affection, as if being called the Lamb of God was as natural as any words of welcome. He offered John the greeting of peace, and I heard him say, "John, I want to be baptized by you." Our cousin protested with words that made me angrier and more confused than before. He was telling Jesus that he couldn't baptize him—"I am not worthy," he said. But Jesus insisted and they approached the water together.

By then everyone had sensed that something extraordinary was happening, and they stood by, transfixed. John cried out, "This is the one of whom I said, 'I am not worthy to untie the thong of his sandal,'" and the crowd hushed and stared.

John lowered Jesus under the water, but as my brother emerged, something occurred that became the talk of John's disciples for quite a while. A strong ray of light broke from the clouds while Jesus stood utterly still as if he were listening. Suddenly, out of nowhere, a dove appeared and perched on his shoulder. Some said they heard a clap of thunder; others that they heard a voice without words. But John told me later that the words were distinct and that both he and Jesus heard them: "This is my Son, the beloved; with you I am well pleased."

The rest is not easy for me to talk about. You know the story. Jesus started on the mission that surprised and worried his family. I well remember the return to Nazareth when he preached with such authority that the people were speechless, and the other time when the crowd went wild over him and we were trying to stop him from his work, thinking he was outside himself. I am so ashamed to remember all our doubts now. But they were there and they were real. When I asked our mother, "What possessed you to call him Savior? Do you not see how he is taking it seriously?" she said, "We were told that this would be his name."

"What do you mean—you were *told*?" I demanded, but she shook her head and her eyes filled with tears. "I never told you children," she said, "but his birth was announced to us from above."

I didn't want to hear any more. I was so filled with doubts about him that I stayed away from him when he was being abused and led like a lamb to the slaughter. My bitterness was overwhelming—first my worry over my mother's grief and then my own despair over the brother I had loved, the one who could have been a great leader but chose the way that led to his death.

I watched everything from afar and, after his burial, I hid to grieve alone. No one knew where I was, not even my mother. And there, one day as I was praying, asking God to forgive me for being unkind to my dead brother, I felt someone standing next to me. When I looked up, I saw it was the Lord, it was Jesus. I recognized him instantly, but his presence made me tremble. He was radiant—he was the Lord. He stretched his hand and I saw the hole on the wrist and cried aloud. But he said, "James, my brother, it is well. Do not be afraid." Afterward, we talked for a long while. My doubts were dispersed, and I promised him I would continue the work he started.

Now, whenever the brothers and sisters refer to me as one of the "pillars of the church," I remember those early years when I knew him only as my brother and I am amazed. Our mother revealed what she had hidden all these years—that all the portents at his birth had prepared her for his life and his death. I am grateful that I was not left without hope at the end—that he came to me as the glorified Lord. He came to me, he forgave me, he did not abandon me. This gives me hope for all those who come after me. Wait, my children, wait for his coming.

Epilogue
The end of one season, the beginning of another

And so we have come together to the end of the thirty-day cycle of waiting for the Wonder. We have heard voices of faith and voices of superstition and violence, voices of a profound belief in something better for a hurting world and voices expressing a desire for what is not apprehended by the senses. We have entered into the wonderful mythos of tradition and legend and the ever-present miracle of faith. We have at times suspended belief in order to feel the sweetness of anticipation. Again and again we have returned to the grounding of the Scriptures.

I hold a strong belief in the doctrine of the Incarnation. The whole edifice of my own life and faith would crumble without this conviction: *I believe in Jesus Christ, the Son of God. . . . He was conceived by the power of the Holy Spirit and born of the Virgin Mary.* The central issue for me is the miracle of God's entering humanity in human form.

I think the eyes and ears of faith are very different from the instruments that make it possible for us to see and hear. Listening to the Christmas story as a child, I used to wonder: *Why is it that the world didn't notice the angels? Why didn't the whole earth resound with the angels' song?* As I was writing these monologues I became convinced that only the ears of faith heard the angels' song, and only the eyes of faith saw the angels, and the one prerequisite for revelation was a heart that longed to see God's goodness on this earth. So it is today.

I became a child again during the imagining of these narrations, but I wrote as an adult who never ignores the mind. I searched the Scriptures assiduously, I searched my own heart and mind, and I entered joyfully into the realm of wonder. For me, Advent is inescapably intertwined with Handel's *Messiah;* as I wrote I heard the words written in the glorious translation of the King James' Version, so perfect for singing, and played the notes of the Handel score in my head.

I look back at the words of the voices in this book and notice that not one of the speakers deals with the possession of material goods or what we call "Christmas presents." I have written with the heart vulnerable and the mind wide open for new possibilities, so I am not surprised that what resulted has nothing to do with what makes up our popular celebration of the season. I hold most dearly the remembrance of my early Advent and Christmas experiences in a very poor country, in Greece during and after World War II, but the memories are filled with so much goodness because we children created all that would go into the season's celebration in our little church those days—the poems and the plays, the songs and the presentations. And that creativity was the greatest gift of all.

So, for all who read these words, I pray for a creative season of entering into the wonder of waiting and the wonder of God's breaking through into our world in the coming of Jesus the Christ. Amen.